What people are saying about ... Alan Coleman's book...

As a voice crying in the wilderness, Apostle Alan Coleman is not afraid to speak the truth with great power and integrity. The Heart of Man and Woman, rules is a must book to read.
Bishop Stanley Lawson
Unity Tabernacle, Kilgore Texas

Apostle Alan Coleman is not only a close friend, but one of the most focused men I have been around. The simple but very profound words in these chapters have changed me. This book offers passion and insight that will launch all who read it.
Pastor Marc Jones
Abundant Harvest Church, Athens Texas

This Book by Apostle Alan Coleman is truly a passionate and motivating message for the Church. The Theme is simple, that we seek the Real Truth, which is the truth of God.
Pastor Sam Cumby, son in the Ministry
Behind the Veil, Fairfield, Texas

The Heart of Man and Woman: Rules The Handbook to Success

By

Alan Coleman, Servant of the Lord

iUniverse, Inc.
New York   Bloomington

iUniverse books may be ordered through booksellers or by contacting:

iUniverse
1663 Liberty Drive
Bloomington, IN 47403
www.iuniverse.com
1-800-Authors (1-800-288-4677)

Because of the dynamic nature of the Internet, any Web addresses or links contained in this book may have changed since publication and may no longer be valid. The views expressed in this work are solely those of the author and do not necessarily reflect the views of the publisher, and the publisher hereby disclaims any responsibility for them.

ISBN: 978-1-4401-6854-3 (sc)
ISBN: 978-1-4401-6856-7 (hc)
ISBN: 978-1-4401-6855-0 (ebook)

Printed in the United States of America

iUniverse rev. date: 11/16/2009

Dedication

First, I'd like to dedicate this book to one of the greatest churches in the world…if you count love. The Gates Community Church Int'l Church in Athens, TX. Thanks Gates for allowing me the time to write.

Secondly, I'd like to thank the best part of me, my wife Elect Lady Ronda Coleman, for all your support and for allowing me the time to write in the midnight hours. Thanks babe.

Thirdly, I'd like to thank my Pastor, Bishop Russell D. Betts for everything he placed in me through the teaching of God's Word. Thanks Pastor.

Lastly, I'd like to thank my mentors in the gospel, Bishop Billy Clark of Hillsboro, TX and Bishop Stanley Lawson of Kilgore, TX for all their Godly advice and for just being true men of God. Thanks again..

Contents

Preface

This book is written for the people who battle everyday situations, not understanding what is really transpiring in their lives. We will be talking about the heart of man and woman, the spiritual computer of mankind. The *Heart* is an important word that some take lightly. Some romantics have written about the heart with deep emotions and warm words. Doctors have written thesis after thesis about this powerful word. Poets described this word with tears pouring out, mixing with ink. The Heart is a powerful word. In the next few chapters, we will read about the heart; not the one that pumps blood but the one that pumps blood to your soul, spiritually.

I write believing that what you read in this book will forever change your life, financially, morally, and certainly spiritually. When you read this book, read it like you've never read scripture before, and God will give you a revelation like never before. Some things you read will cause you to question, but keep reading because God is at work. You may be a Christian, Muslim, or atheist, and that's fine, but I promise after reading this book, everything will change for the better. Enjoy.

Chapter 1
What Has Been Taught about the Heart?

In the scriptures, the Greek word *kardia* means a physical heart, but only in reference to the importance of the spiritual heart. The spiritual heart does not sit in your chest but in your head or between the ears, as my old professor would say. Throughout the Old and New Testament, the Bible speaks about the heart of man. In Jeremiah 17:10 I, it says, "The Lord search the heart. I try the reins, even to give every man according to his ways, and according to the fruit of his doings." Mark 7:20–23 states, "That which cometh out of the man, that defileth the man. For from within, out of the heart of men, proceed evil thoughts, adulteries, fornications, murders, thefts, covetousness, wickedness, deceit, lasciviousness, and evil eye, blasphemy, pride, foolishness: All these evil things come from within, and defile the man."

When we look at the prophet Jeremiah and our savior Jesus, they are speaking of a problem not on the outside, but on the inside, in the heart.

God really looks at the heart, but man looks at the outward appearance. In 1 Samuel 16:7, it states, "But the LORD said unto Samuel, 'Look not on his countenance, or on the height of his stature; because I have refused him': for the LORD seeth not as man seeth; for man looketh on the outward appearance, but the LORD looketh on the heart." We as people always look at the outer surface rather than seeking the true inner being. But God looks at the inner being first, because that's where everything starts and eventually ends.

The heart is a place that only God knows totally. So people will even say, "No one knows my heart except God." And that is true until you speak. Matthew 12:34: "O generation of vipers, how can ye, being evil, speak good things? For out of the abundance of the heart, the mouth speaketh." Our heart contains all the truths as we know them, and whenever we speak, they will eventually flow out. Have you ever noticed that you can be speaking to someone about religion or politics and it will not be long before that person's beliefs are flowing out like water? What is in the heart will surely flow, sooner rather than later. The heart occasionally fools man, but eventually the real truth flows out of it. There used to be a saying that a leopard could hide it spots for about six months, seemingly resembling a lion, but after that period, the cub would stop looking like a lion and start looking like a leopard. That's the way the heart performs sometimes; it tries to resemble other type of hearts, but eventually the truth that's in it oozes out due to the *works of the body* yielding to it. I will explain later about the body yielding to the heart.

Saul had been turned down by God, and he warned Samuel not to get caught up in worrying about how a king ought to look. In the Old Testament days, the countries sought tall, handsome, and broad-shouldered men to be kings.

But as Samuel sought a king, God sent him to a ruddy man, who was after God's heart. 1 Samuel 13:14: "But now thy kingdom shall not continue: the LORD hath sought him a man after his own heart, and the LORD hath commanded him to be captain over his people, because thou hast not kept that which the LORD commanded thee."

What does it mean to be after God's heart? Well it means that David chased God's heart. How can you chase after God's heart? God's heart is a heart filled with the truth, and David sought to have a heart just like God's. Certainly, this is a powerful statement: to chase after God's heart. But that is the heart of God for all: to love him enough to want to be just like him. You've seen sons try to emulate their fathers. Guess what? That's exactly what God seeks from us. In Genesis, God tells us that we were made in his image. On the inside, we are just like God: spirit. But just like a baby, as we feed on food, we become stronger each day, favoring our parents each day, until eventually we look quite like them. We are the same way spiritually. As we feed on the word (truth), we favor our father each and every day. If we are not careful, we will look like, talk like, and even smell like our savior, Jesus. That's what King David strived to do. No, he was not perfect, but he strived to be like the heart of God. Remember the scripture Psalm 119:11: "Thy word have I hid in mine heart, that I might not sin against thee." Here, David has vowed to place the word in his heart, *because whatever truth is in the heart, the body will eventually manifest.* David wanted to have a heart like God's even though he was imperfect; he continually sought God. Remember Hebrews 11:6: "But without faith, it is impossible to please him: for he that cometh to God must believe that he is, and that he is a rewarder of them that diligently *seek* him." When we seek him, we will surely find him. How do we find him? We find him in the truth, the word. The word of God is awesome. All of the words of God fit together like a glove to accomplish an appointed end.

Moreover, we pursue him day after day, dying to self to be more like Jesus. 1 Cor 15:31: "I protest by your rejoicing, which I have in Christ Jesus our Lord, I die daily." Paul speaks of himself dying to flesh daily for the sake of Christ. The more we die of worldly truths, fleshly truths, and also truths of the devil, the more we die daily. And if the truth be said, *all these truths make us the people we are.* And if we have been living according to the truths of the world, the truths of Satan, and even our own truths, we have been living a lie, because our lives are based on false truths. I once preached a sermon titled "A Schizophrenic Mind." It was based on people living lives out of their true character, thus living helter-skelter lives. And in this rat race, nothing seems to work correctly. People are seeking relationships instead of intimacy with God, and many men and women work their entire lives only to finally accept that their lives as empty. Our true character is to *have God's character*, thus causing us to enjoy the true purpose of life. In saying this, let's examine the gist of this book.

The heart of man is the CPU of the man, for you computer gurus. Remember Computers 101: garbage in, garbage out. The Greek word for "heart" is *kardías*, which is the seat and center of human life.[1] The reason Jesus compares the spiritual heart with the physical heart is that even when your kidneys and your liver are functioning properly, none of that matters if the heart stops. When the heart stops, everything else shuts down. Well, Jesus is saying the same for the spiritual heart, which is between your ears. When that heart goes bad, so does the physical body. So our savior puts emphasis on the heart. Keep it pure, Matthew

5:8 states, "Blessed are the pure in heart: for they shall see God." This is encouraging. And how would anyone purify his heart? The only way the heart can be purified is by pure things. And the only pure thing we know is Jesus, the truth. So we have to place the truth or the word in our hearts to purify them. I believe the importance of this scripture is not only seeing God in eternity, but *right now,* while in the land of the living. "I had fainted, unless I had believed to see the goodness of the LORD in the land of the living" (Psalm 27:13). Notice that Matthew 5:8 is not saying that the others—v. 3, the poor; v. 4, the mourning; v. 5, the meek, or even v. 7, the merciful—will not see God in eternity. No, of course not. But blessed are the pure in heart; for they shall see God then and now. Why now? Well how many needed him in that last fight with the enemy or in that last marriage or even with that rebellious child? We need him then and now.

All throughout scripture, men and women of God sought God in battle. Jeremiah sought God in battle. "Thou art my battle axe and weapons of war: for with thee will I break in pieces the nations, and with thee will I destroy kingdoms" (Jeremiah 51:20). Jeremiah said God is a battle axe. Now God can be a battle axe all he wants, but unless you pick him up, the axe is useless for you.

So how do we get a pure heart? Obviously you can't pour pureness in and you can't work for it, as that contradicts the word of God. This will be the topic of this book.

The heart is a place where only truths sit. I think this is important, as we must explain *truth.* Truth is just as important as the heart itself. Webster's states truth is "the quality or state of being true; agreement with a standard or rule." Everyone wants it and everyone hunts for it, but what is it? Truth is simply a thought concluded. When we think about anything and finally conclude whether that thing is right or wrong, we have just made a decision and this equates to truth. Here's an example. Someone may say, "Hey, did you hear about Jake? They said he cheated on his wife." Now you know Jake, and he is a powerful man of God. You may ponder this and finally say, "No way." What happened during that process? You thought about it and concluded that what you heard was a lie. Every one of us faces thoughts like these daily. And our hearts are waiting for truths to fill it daily. That's why the heart of man is critical to life, and this is the chemistry of the heart. Again, the heart is a place where only truths sit. Now, some will say, "Wait, do you mean the only thing that can be in the heart is truth?" The answer is yes, truth as you know it.

Let me give a quick example. I will speak hypothetically. Let's say you are looking at a piece of carpet that is blue, but you have an audience there, and these people are acquaintances except for one. For some reason, you are trying to convince them that the carpet is red. Let's say the one person that wasn't an acquaintance was forcing you to make this statement. Now the people you know will first think you're kidding, of course. But they know you and they see frustration on your face, so finally they say, "Yes, it's red." Some agreed because they were impatient. Now even though they agreed, they still know that carpet is blue. The point is that they knew that it was blue. The heart only accepts truths as it know it, even when the mouth says different.

Let me give another example, fictional of course. My deacon gave me a watch and he said it was eighteen-karat gold. I was excited because I had faith (*pistis*, belief in a truth) in this deacon, so I was proud to wear it. Everywhere I went, I somehow ended up checking the time, especially when someone was looking. I walked with confidence because in my heart I had a truth: that this watch was expensive and eighteen-karat gold. But later that year, my wife wanted a 2008 Porsche, and I needed ten thousand dollars for a down payment and I had only six thousand dollars. So I thought I would run to the pawn shop and surely they would give me four thousand dollars for the watch. When I got there, they said the watch was worth fifteen. I quickly ran out of the pawn shop, as I felt the manager was trying to cheat me. So I drove fifty miles to by best friends' pawn shop to let him in on this steal of a deal. I entered with confidence and said, "Mark, I want to get a loan on this eighteen-karat-gold watch."

He examined it and asked, "How much do you want for it?"

I told him, "Oh, about four thousand dollars." He laughed, and I asked why.

He said, "Brother, this watch is worth about fifteen dollars." I dropped my head and walked away. My heart had been fooled. It was fooled by a truth: not *the* truth, but *a* truth. The heart only receives what the person believes to be true.

Thus far, we covered the heart and what it consists of, stating that the only thing the heart will receive is truth as you know it. Now, when a thought enters the mind—the mind surrounds the heart—and when the mind ponders a thing, it comes to a conclusion, deciding if that thing is true or not. This conclusion is the truth as that person knows it, and that truth settles in the heart. Thus your body now submits itself to the truth. The flesh has to submit to the heart. God created man that way. *Our heart rules, whether it's a bad one or pure one.* As you can see, the heart is extremely important. It is the center of man. In the book of James, God speaks of three enemies of man: first, the world; second, Satan; and third, you. Let's enter in a little deeper.

Each believer is responsible for the condition of his heart: "My son, forget not my law (truth); but let thine heart keep my commandments" (Proverbs 3:1). We see a direct connection between walking the word out and what truths are in the heart. We serve God with our heart or mind. Our heart drives us to good works or it drives us to evil works or sin. How do we let our heart keep God's commandments? There's just one way, and that is by putting *the truth* of God in our hearts. That is the only way we can let the heart keep God's word. Man was created for the word of God. We were built for it. Our spirit yearns for it, whether we know it or not. Many go to their graves not knowing this intrinsic truth. But God admonishes us that we should seek him.

Have you ever purchased a toaster, a bicycle, or even a cell phone? All these products come with manuals to show you the way to assemble or operate them. Why would they need manuals? The company supplies these manuals to show you how to get the most out of the product. On one occasion, I purchased a bicycle for my daughter, and it was unassembled. Being a college graduate and renowned author, I cast the pamphlet in the trash. After starting this simplistic task and having the bicycle halfway assembled, I noticed I had to place the brakes on. I had to place them on before the wheel was attached. Well, guess what? I had already put on the wheel. So I had to take the bike almost totally apart to attach the brakes. I looked over in the trash and read the pamphlet, and of course the instructions said to place the brakes on first. Now if I had read the instructions, my job would have been easier. This analogy is the same for man. God is the creator, and he has a manual on how man operates. The manual even tells us what we can't do with some products. For instance, you wouldn't take a toaster and try to clean it in the dishwasher, would you? Certainly not; the toaster wasn't designed to be cleaned like that, and the manual states unequivocally not to put it in water. The Bible is the same way. It warns us what not to do, and the Bible also admonishes us about what to do. But even though the toaster manual explains explicitly to keep it away from water, many people are harmed each year by letting water come into contact with appliances. When we don't follow instructions, only bad things happen. Again, it's the same with the Bible. Many read it but still try to do things that the body is not built to handle, and there are dire consequences. So, *the truth* is of paramount importance to the heart.

Thus, the heart is the foundation of man, and the enemy knows this. That is why he attacks the heart aggressively each and every day, blow after blow and sometimes chip after chip. With time, a slow drip of water can tear down a mountain, and the enemy exercises these skills with perfection. He focuses on the heart, knowing if he can gain even 1 percent a year, he's fine. And then he stakes his ground in victory, because he knows it's the start of devastation. The enemy's whole aim is to keep darkness or ignorance prevalent, to set snares for the men and women. He banks that this strategy will work. "When the enemy shall come in like a flood, the Spirit of the LORD shall lift up a standard against him. And the Redeemer shall come to Zion, and unto them that turn from transgression in Jacob, saith the LORD" (Isaiah 59:19). The enemy has a plan, but so does God. God is stronger than the enemy and smarter than the enemy, so why get caught in a snare that has been premeasured just for you? A loving God is trying to convey to you to lend him your heart, even if you do not want to give it completely. Watch God move in that trial season, and I promise you will totally give your heart to him.

We can't make our own hearts clean or clean anyone else's. God cleans the heart with his word (Jesus). Let's look at scripture. "Who can say, 'I have made my heart clean, I am pure from my sin'?" (Proverbs 20:9). Man cannot clean his own heart with his own truth. Only God cleans a man's heart, and he cleans it with Jesus. The word is God's primary weapon against the enemy. *The word offers light where there's darkness and strength where there's weakness.* The word feeds the heart with the heartbeat of truth. This truth beats the lies of the enemy out of that important spiritual organ.

The enemy uses false truths on men and women of God daily. The enemy wants man to take that day of judgment as a normal day in today's court system. But believe me, men and women, this will be a day like never seen before. We on earth have never seen a true judge before. I will give a quick example. The toughest or strictest judge you know still has some leniency. For instance, if a judge's golf buddy's son committed a crime or got into some minor trouble, even this judge may give him stern talk but would show some leniency. But on this day, Jesus will not be a savior but a true judge, evaluating everyone according to their works. On this day, no mercy will be shown. The mercy is being shown now, every time someone tells you God cares or looks for you in church or tells you about God. But today's thought is simply, don't worry; God understands. He's a merciful God. He knows you're human. This lie is even in the kingdom of God right now. But men and women, judgment is coming, according to 2 Cor 5:10–11, Rev. 22:12, Rv 1:3, and Rv 22:7. There are many more scriptures that lead us to this truth. Don't let the destroyer fool you; he's not as crafty as he thinks. It really is a crazy thing that he's been using the same lies and tricks since he was cast out of heaven.

We have to give him credit, though. This enemy has fought Adam, Elijah, David, Isaiah, Mark, Matthew, and even Jesus. The devil is not omniscient like God, but he has longevity. Thus, I believe that at our birth, the enemy watches how we walk, talk, and even eat. And I believe he concludes, "This man walks like King David," or, "This woman talks like Debra, the prophetess." Sometimes he sees how we think. That's right: how we think. How can anyone tell how you think? They watch what you do and how you do it. This counterfeiter knows how to impede or even completely stop the flow of God in our lives. He contrives snares to pull us from our destiny, placing people in our lives who would be albatrosses instead of blessings to help us to our destiny. The enemy uses people as friends and partners or even soul mates to infiltrate our lives.

We have to be careful who we let into our lives. I teach that a husband or wife enters our lives to help us in our destiny, not to delay our destiny or goals in Christ. The Bible said the wife is a help meet. The wife helps the husband, and the husband helps the wife. That is why God's truth is so important. "Be ye not unequally yoked together with unbelievers: for what fellowship hath righteousness with unrighteousness?" (2 Cor 6:14). God didn't put this scripture in for good reading, but because God knows what's best for us. Our destinies in Christ are important to God, because those destinies are often important to people we don't even know. God has high places waiting, but many times our flesh or false truths have us preoccupied. Before long our lives are exhausted without us ever grasping the destiny God has provided. In that sense, the enemy has prevailed. But for those of you who are seventy or older, remember that Moses' ministry didn't start until he was eighty. I say this because as long as you have breath in your body, God can do it in you. Never give up, even if you are sick. Ask God to raise you up to where you can finish what he started. Tell God you have him in your heart and the devil is in trouble. Now let's explore the power of the truth in our hearts.

Chapter 2
Belief

For truth to be truth as we know it, there must be belief. The Greek word for *believe* also means "commit unto." The verb πείθω means "to persuade, to cause belief, to induce one to do something by persuading," and so it runs into the meaning of *obey*. The New Testament talks about believing, but most people, including church people, think believing means that something or someone exists. This is not what the scriptures teach. Let me give you an example. Once, before anyone came into the church, I eased in and placed a ten dollar bill under a vase on the stage in the church. When service started, I began preaching about believing, and I looked at my wife in service and said, "Babe, there is a ten dollar bill under that vase. Would you get it?" and I kept on preaching. Now there was no reason why a ten dollar bill should be under the vase. So my wife looked at me and kept on doing what she was doing. Then I told my armor bearer, "There is a ten bill under the vase." Immediately, he jumped up and looked under the vase. Now what was the difference between the two? Well one believed and the other didn't, for whatever reason. One did something, and the other did not. What did one do? Well, he got up and looked.

The New Testament teaches us to believe, and Jesus personally taught people to believe. When he was telling the Pharisees, "Believe in me and you shall not perish," he was not saying, "Believe that I am here in front of you, that I exist." They were looking at him; they knew he existed. But Jesus was telling the Pharisees to believe what he was saying: the truth. Remember, if you believe what he's saying, you will get up and look under the vase. Belief always bring a response.

Realistically, belief and obedience are close synonyms. Look at Acts 5:32: "We are his witnesses of these things; and *so is* also the Holy Ghost, whom God hath given to them that obey him." The word *obey* means "to follow the commands or guidance." You can go through the New Testament and interchangeably use *obey* and *believe* in the scriptures, because when you obey willing, you believe. When you believe, you obey. They have to be used closely. You cannot say you believe but then disobey; it's impossible. You cannot obey willing and not believe. God just made us like that. This goes to the heart of this book.

All Jesus wanted them to do was believe him. Guess what? All Jesus wants us to do is believe him now, because if you believe him, you will do what he says. John 8:51 says, "Verily, verily, I say unto you, If a man keep my saying, he shall never see death (second death)."

So how do you believe? First, you must have something to believe. There are four entities trying to deliver something to believe: the world, the devil, you, and Jesus, the living word. Men have a choice of what truth to believe. God doesn't force us to receive his truth. He lets you decide. But he does say in Deut 30:19, "I call heaven and earth to record this day against you, that I have set before you life and death, blessing and cursing:

therefore choose life." Truth brings life and blessings, but lies or false truths bring curses and death. Therefore, there is a direct correlation between believing and salvation. Romans 10:10 says, "For with the heart man believeth unto righteousness; and with the mouth confession is made unto salvation. What do man believeth to equate to righteousness?" The truth, Jesus the Christ, is the answer and not *a* truth. The Greek word for *righteousness* means, in a broad sense, "state of him who is as he ought to be, righteousness, the condition acceptable to God; the doctrine concerning the way in which man may attain a state approved of God; integrity, virtue, purity of life, rightness, correctness of thinking feeling, and acting." In a narrower sense, it means "justice or the virtue which gives each his due."[2] So when you believe the truth, the body or works follow accordingly and the belief produces righteousness. The body or the works of the body have no choice but to submit to the heart. So whatever truth is in the heart, this is what man has become.

Belief equates with righteousness—not any belief, but the belief in the truth, Jesus. I explain righteousness as being kind of like the stop signs in a city. Whenever you stop at a sign, the police equate that to righteousness in that city. But when you decide not to stop—maybe you're just in a hurry—the policeman will stop you and give you a ticket because you ignored the law or the sign, thus being unrighteous. The power of believing is tremendous for the kingdom. As a matter of fact, without it, no man can obtain the kingdom of God. Let's talk now about how faith belongs in this teaching.

Chapter 3
Faith

Faith, in the Greek, means (pistis) conviction or belief in a truth of anything. The conviction or belief in a truth—that is what faith means. Why is faith explained a believing in *a* truth and not *the* truth? The reason why is that you can have faith in things other than God—*a* truth. Just look around; people all over the world have faith in something. What about those who worship Buddha or Allah, or even those who worship Satan. Do they not have faith? Sure they do, just as much as you. I didn't blaspheme; read on. Many feel that Hebrews 11:1 explains what faith means, but instead it explains an example of faith. The Greek word *pistis* means a conviction or belief in a truth. Consequently, people who believe in things or religions other than what you have faith in still have faith. There are a lot of people with faith walking on this earth. The big question is, what is their faith in?

A while ago, I preached a message about judgment day. I preached about how even those in the church will stand in judgment before Jesus. He won't be a savior now but a judge. As 2 Cor 5:10 says, "For we must all appear before the judgment seat of Christ; that every one may receive the things done in his body, according to that he hath done, whether it be good or bad." The

Lord gave me revelation in which he showed me that some will stand before Christ and he will tell them, "I never knew you."

Some will say, "But I had faith, big faith, Jesus."

Then, Jesus will grab his binoculars and focus on that mountain of faith. He will say, "You sure did. That's big faith." Next he will tell Gabriel, "Give me that shovel. I'm going to see what truth that faith was in." (Without truth, faith is null and void). Jesus will state, "Your faith was in *a* truth, but not *the* truth. The truth is my truth or my word. I don't know you!" That's a sentence no one wants to hear. Thomas Hobbes, an English philosopher, produced a writing titled "Hell is Truth Seen Too Late." This writing had very little to do with Jesus, but the statement is profound. That is really what hell is: the truth, too late. Hell is a place where men and women will find the truth; it will just be too late.

Some churches teach faith is this hard sought out word that is difficult to obtain, or some teach that it is a simple entity. If you just believe that he exists, you have it. Even demons know or believe he exists. James 2:19 says, "Thou believest that there is one God; thou doest well: the devils also believe, and tremble." So faith is neither hard nor easy, but man has to sift through many false truths in life to find it. But be not discouraged, because God says he gives a measure of faith. Romans 12:3 states, "According as God hath dealt to every man the measure of faith." God gives a measurement of belief to gather the truth. The functioning factors of the spiritual heart are faith, belief, and truth. They all work together for its betterment or for its demise.

So all the scriptures that speak about faith are realistically speaking of believing in a truth. Let's look at Hebrews 10:38 closely: "Now the just shall live by faith: but if *any man* draw back, my soul shall have no pleasure in him." The scripture simply says those that have been justified live by believing in the truth, and because they believe in the truth, they're justified. Remember the statement earlier that if you believe, you obey, and if you obey willingly, you believe. Now let's look at Hebrews 10:38: "The just shall live by obeying or believing the truth, but if any man draw back …" draw back from what? Draw back from believing or obeying the truth. When we understand faith as Jesus wanted us to understand it, it brings a new revelation and love toward him. Let's look at Romans 14:23: "For whatsoever *is* not of faith is sin." Let's inject the Greek meaning in the scripture: "For whatsoever is disobeying or not believing the truth is sin as God knows it."

As Paul generalized, *everything that does not come from (ek,* "out of") *faith is sin.* The principle is, "When in doubt, don't." The strong Christian (Paul 15:1) is wrong if he causes a weak brother to sin by doing something while doubting (Paul 14:20), and a weak brother (v. 1–2) who goes against what he doubts also sins (v. 23).[3]

Let's look at one more scripture. Luke 18:8 says, "I tell you that he will avenge them speedily. Nevertheless when the Son of man cometh, shall he find faith on the earth?"[4] Shall he find *obeying* or *believing* on the earth? Believing or obeying what? Believing or obeying the truth of Jesus the Christ. Truth is what is true as you know it and as you believe it.

Nicodemus didn't understand how a man could be born again, meaning physical birth. But Jesus meant spiritual birth or how a man's *heart* could be born again. John 3:15–16 says, "That whosoever believeth in him should not perish, but have eternal life. For God so loved the world, that he gave his only begotten Son, that whosoever believeth in him should not perish, but have everlasting life." There is that word again, *believeth* (believe or obey). Jesus is speaking face-to-face with Nicodemus; Jesus is not telling Nicodemus, "If you believe I am standing in front of you or that I exist, you shall not perish." He is telling him to believe him, not only that Jesus is the son of God but that everything that's coming out of his mouth is true. Remember, what we believe to be true sits in our hearts as a truth. So, if man believes in Jesus and believes that he is the son of God and believes what he says is truth, he shall not perish or experience the second death. There is a direct correlation between a heart being filled with the truth and entering the kingdom of God.

Chapter 4
Truth

The World

The first enemy of the heart that we will talk about is this world. People all over the world have sought out truth. Even great philosophers have strained and stretched to gain the ultimate truth. Socrates yearned for truth, as supposedly he had it all but would only share it in conversation. He wouldn't write it down, so the only way you could receive it was to converse with him. What does truth mean? Some say whatever is true is truth. Leo Tolstoy wrote, "Wrong does not cease to be wrong because the majority share in it." Leo was absolutely right; just because the numbers are on the side of wrong doesn't make it right.

Truth is a powerful word that is so misunderstood among this society. But even in history, Socrates, Nietzsche, Schopenhauer, and Descartes processed and reprocessed truth and still lacked it. But the truth this book is talking about is *the Truth*. John 14:6 : "Jesus saith unto him, 'I am the way, *the truth*, and the life: no man cometh unto the Father, but by me.'" This truth is paramount to the heart; lest this truth is pondered, it cannot enter the heart. In scripture after scripture, God impresses truth upon us. Why harp on truth in book after book of the Bible? Why speak through Old and New Testament saints to echo truth to mankind? And the answer is simply that God knew the way he created man, and he loved man with all of his heart and created us as spiritual beings. 2 Peter 3:9: "The Lord is not slack concerning his promise, as some men count slackness; but is longsuffering to usward, not willing that any should perish, but that all should come to repentance." Truth is anything we called true, that we believe. See, no matter how powerful truth is, God wants to see how you view it. There are truths everywhere, and I mean everywhere. What do you call truth? There is *a* truth, and there is *the* truth. There is a difference between the two. For example, some people believe roaches are nasty useless insects. That is a truth in the United States, but in many countries, these insects are considered a delicacy and are rich in protein and low in fat. So, "Roaches are nasty, useless insects" is just *a* truth, not *the* truth. So what seems to be truth is not always absolute truth.

Real truth is the truth of God, and all through the scriptures he conveys that. Deuteronomy 32:4: "He is the Rock, his work is perfect: for all his ways are judgment: a God of truth and without iniquity, just and right is he." Here, God shows us his love, that he is a God of *the* truth, not *a* truth. All of my life, I thought I knew what truth was. But like you, I was pressed on every side by truths everywhere. Now if you are still reading this book, you probably know that when you was born into this world, the ways of this world weighed on you. And even though you were conceived in sin, you are not sin or born into sin. There is a difference. Psalms 51:5 states, "Behold, I was shapen in iniquity; and in sin did my mother *conceive* me." Again, this world poured its truths on you from day one, including the way to talk and even the way to walk. Life challenges us in our daily walks. The environment is adding to our growth daily. Of course, we realize nature is adding a part, too. Some curses carry over in blood lines, causing taste buds that lead some to immorality. Simply put, some are more apt to drink or to try drugs and get caught in the trap of the enemy; these are examples of nature. But when it comes to our spiritual environment, nurture plays a huge role.

Proverbs 13:20 says, "He that walketh with wise men shall be wise: but a companion of fools shall be destroyed." In 1 Cor 15:33, it says, "Be not deceived: evil communications corrupt good manners." Bad company corrupts good morals. Family can even play an important role here. I remember when I was about thirteen—you know, the age where you're not worrying or thinking about girls. I was playing basketball, which was the thing to do back when I was a kid. My family wasn't rich, but we never wanted for much. One of the players on the basketball team was a young girl about my age. And you remember when you were a kid and you thought girls were just like boys. Well this day, my cousin, who was an adult in age only, said, "Hey, cuz, come here. What's that babe's name?"

I said, "What babe?" as I scoped the court.

He said, "That one there."

I said, "BJ, short for Betty Jean. Oh, she's one of the guys."

My cousin said, "Cuz, she's hot."

I said, "Her?"

He said, "Sure, cuz." He said, "You haven't hit that yet?"

I said, "Hit it? What are you talking about?" Then I realized, and I said, "No, she just one of the boys." Then for the first time, I really looked at BJ, and I didn't see the little basketball girl; I saw something hot. My cousin had implanted truth as he saw it, and I agreed. This is definitely how lust starts. What truth did my cousin bestow upon me? A truth that at my age, I should be dating and having sex, not doing what young teenage boys should be doing: enjoying being a teenager. And I pondered it and finally believed it. So my heart had received a truth: not *the* truth, but *a* truth.

Truths lurk everywhere, even in premises of falsehood. This world has all types of truth. The philosopher Karl Marx stated, "Catch a man a fish, and you can sell it to him. Teach a man to fish, and you ruin a wonderful business opportunity." Selfishness at it best. The Book of James 3:15 states, "This wisdom descendeth not from above, but is earthly, sensual, devilish." In other words, selfishness comes from the pit of hell. But yet the world teaches this truth to affect the heart of man. Remember, the only thing that can sit in the heart is truth. The secular world now teaches right to be wrong and wrong to be right. Jesus warned us of this even in the kingdom of God. As 2 Timothy 4:3–4 states, "For the time will come when they will not endure sound doctrine; but after their own lusts shall they heap to themselves teachers, having itching ears; And they shall turn away their ears from the truth, and shall be turned unto fables." The truths of this world lure men and women away from the truth of God. *Truth is anything we call true, that we believe.* The philosopher Nietzsche stated, "Believe me! The secret of reaping the greatest fruitfulness and the greatest enjoyment from life is to live dangerously!" Remember, the heart only receives truth as you know it and believe it. Nietzsche spoke in his own words, stated truth as he knew and believed it. He felt the greatest fruitfulness and the greatest enjoyment in life was to live dangerously. He believed it; thus this truth sat in his heart. The consequence was that Nietzsche worked out what was in his heart. His body worked out what was implanted in his heart, guaranteed.

Years ago, I had a best friend who I grew up with who was a real okay guy. I grew up in and out of church, but this friend's family wasn't what we called churchgoers. One day, he confided in me and told me he was gay. I said out of amazement, "Naw, I saw you talking to Jane, and what about Lisa?"

He said, "I was just blending in."

I was hurt, but I felt sorry for him, as I knew how gay men were treated in those days. Then I asked, "How Jeff?"

He stated, "I believe I was born like this." Then he said, "After I heard this guy on television stating he was born like this, I concluded that God does make some men to love men, or that God makes some mistakes." Then he said he read a commentary on alternative lifestyles. So he said, "I feel comfortable about it now. I used to feel shame, and when I did go to church, I felt guilty about it." Even as I write this book, oh how I pray that I had known then what I know now. See, this friend was not a bad kid or even a bad person. He was just a person who believed a truth, and because he believed it, it sat in his heart, and because it was in his heart, his body finally surrendered. The funny thing is, he said that in the beginning, he just thought about it, but he didn't do it. He said he had always heard it was wrong. My friend had had a truth in his heart, and the truth was that it was wrong to engage in homosexual behavior. But another thought entered his mind, and he concluded that it was true, thus it fell in his heart. Then it was just a matter of time before he was walking it out.

Jesus speaks about this through his apostle, James. James 1:14–15 states, "But every man is tempted, when he is drawn away of his own lust, and enticed. Then when lust hath conceived, it bringeth forth sin: and sin, when it is finished, bringeth forth death." In the Greek, this use of *death* means "the second death." As you read this book you're probably come to a conclusion that truth is pertinent to a pure heart, and this conclusion would be absolutely true and lifesaving.

The world plays a huge role in the condition of the heart. But as long as we are here, we have to understand we are *in* the world, but certainly not *of* this world. So we have to learn how to function in the world with the truth of God. This is why God has the church, *ekklesia*, called-out ones. He called us from the world, but not out of the world, to be light in a dark world.

Chapter 5
Satan

The next enemy of the heart that we will discuss is Satan himself. He is one of the most notorious foes of the heart. He knows the heart is the key, even to salvation. Romans 10:10 states, "For with the heart man believeth unto righteousness; and with the mouth confession is made unto salvation." So he's throwing lies non-stop, as a man would throw mud upon a wall and pray that some will stick. Since we realize that the heart's nucleus is truth, we should be willing only the truth to impregnate our hearts. Jesus speaks on Satan and his truths as he rebukes the Pharisees in John 8:44, "Ye are of your father the devil, and the lusts of your father ye will do. He was a murderer from the beginning, and abode not in the truth, because there is no truth in him. When he speaketh a lie, he speaketh of his own: for he is a liar, and the father of it."

All through scripture God speaks of truth, in which he is. The word for *light* in the Greek also indicates knowledge, and the word for *darkness* also indicates ignorance. *God brings knowledge and truth, but Satan brings ignorance and lies.* Satan wants you to believe a lie. He even tried it on the son of God himself, as seen in Matthew 4:8–9: "Again, the devil taketh him up into an exceeding high mountain, and sheweth him all the kingdoms of the world, and the glory of them; And saith unto him, 'All these things will I give thee, if thou wilt fall down and worship me.'" If the enemy would tempt Jesus, he surely will tempt us. Satan again uses darkness to blind even the kingdom of God. But his main focus is on those who do not know the truth or those who know little. His hope is to pick off a few at a time. Have you ever seen programs on television in which lions or cheetahs, when they seek their prey, try to pick out the weakling of the group? The lion knows he can't catch the entire herd at once, but just the weakest, the slowest, the clumsiest of them all. Satan is the same way; he preys on the ignorant, the proud, and the ones who have no idea of what's going on spiritually. He sets traps and snares to gather his prey. He wounds and kills until he has had his fill, and that is never. His hope is to emulate God and to fool man into believing he is serving the true and living God. All along, man would be serving Satan. He is a foe of man indeed.

True Light

Jesus is light and knowledge, and Satan is darkness and lies. Jesus tells us he is the only light other than ourselves when we have truth in us. John 8:12 says, "Then spake Jesus again unto them, saying, 'I am the light of the world: he that followeth me shall not walk in darkness, but shall have the light of life.'" Jesus even told the disciples in John 11:9–10 that if you walk in the light, you will not stumble, but if you walk in the dark, you shall stumble. He's telling the disciples, "If you walk in truth, you shall not stumble or fall in sin. But if you walk in darkness, or if you walk in lies or false truths, you shall fall into sin." Why? Your body shall follow whatever truths are in your heart. So Jesus continually presses upon us that he is the truth. There is no other on earth, only the son of God. That is *the* truth we have to believe, lest our actions suffer.

In John 3:19, it says, "And this is the condemnation, that light is come into the world, and men loved darkness rather than light, because their deeds were evil." The light, or Jesus, in a sense causes condemnation. Why? The light gives us a choice: light or darkness. Men love darkness or false truths because of their fleshly ways or deeds. The light or truth will show them their faults, themselves. I've learned over the years that men and women do not really want to see themselves. That's why many wear masks to cover their real faces and hide in their sins or faults. But this cycle condemns; that's why Jesus came to deliver us not only from the world and Satan but from ourselves.

So many people hide behind masks, even in church. The sin has trapped them and even intimidated them so they won't come out. The sin brings shame and embarrassment. I once preached a revival, and the Lord moved mightily each night. But one night, the altar was full. Men and women clustered at the altar, and a young lady who I presumed was ready to accept Jesus wholeheartedly came running to the altar. So I asked her, "Are you ready to receive the Lord Jesus as your Lord?" She said yes, and I said, "Are you willing to repent from the ways of the world and turn to the ways of the kingdom of God, as stated in 2 Peter 3:9?"

She said, "Well I'm living with a man who's not my husband. He helps me pay bills and take care of my children."

I said, "The way of the kingdom of God is to marry this man if you want to be with him." Her remark was that he refuses to be with one woman. I told her Jesus was asking to be her husband now and he would take care of her children and also take care of her. I explained, "If this man loved you, he would marry you."

She said, "You don't understand," and walked off. Now the normal way many have offered Jesus as a savior is to quote Romans 10:9, which is a perfect scripture. We say something like, "Repeat this scripture after me," and when they do, we tell them that they are now saved. This woman was still with the man who was not her husband, still living in sin, and didn't understand how to come out. This person would have left with a false sense of being saved.

This is how many will enter hell through the church. But the scripture really has to be broken down and explained. To believe in your heart, the CPU between your ears, is to have the truth of God in your heart. This simply means believing that what Jesus said is true and being able to say that Jesus is Lord. That means you have agreed to obey him. This young lady was willing to accept Jesus as her savior, but not as her Lord. They both must go together. She wasn't agreeable to letting that man go. She decided to keep him and wait for Christ.

Remember the rich man in Matthew 19:24? Jesus offered him salvation, but he decided to keep the riches rather than accept obedience. This scripture wasn't about being rich. The blessings of the Lord will make you rich and add no sorrow according to Proverbs 10:22. This was about obedience. The rich man walked away; he chose the kingdom of this world over the kingdom of God. Salvation, believe or not, is about choice, remember Deut 30:19: "I place before you life and death. Choose life that you and your children may live." Salvation is about living, not dying, and it is a choice. People can't make us accept Jesus as Lord. We have to want life instead of death. But how can anyone know this unless they hear a preacher? Romans 10:17: "So then faith *cometh* by hearing, and hearing by the word of God." Let's break down this scripture, partially in the Greek. Or faith (belief in a truth, Pistis Gk.) cometh by hearing, and hearing by the word (truth) of God. The key to salvation is Jesus being your Lord. Remember, whoever you obey is your Lord. If you obey the ways of this world, that means this world is your Lord. If you obey Jesus the Christ, then Jesus is your Lord. It is impossible to have Jesus as your Lord if you do not obey him. Luke 6:46 states, "And why call ye me, Lord, Lord, and do not the things which I say? But he that heareth and doeth not, is like a man that without a foundation built a house upon the earth; against which the stream did beat vehemently, and immediately it fell; and the ruin of that house was great" (Luke 6:49). Many will say, "I love you Jesus," but their hearts are far from Jesus. Their hearts are filled with false truths and outright lies, thus causing them to be far from Jesus. Our hearts have to be filled with the truth (Jesus) if we want to be with Jesus. Our light has to shine, when *the Light* is in our hearts.

In John 12:46, Jesus tells us that he comes to be a light in the world, that "whosoever believeth in me should not abide in darkness." When we receive the true light, we cannot stay in darkness or lies and false truths. That is why when we stay in darkness and say we know the light, we are liars and the truth is not in us—Jesus is not in us. As 1 John 2:4 says, "He that saith, I know him, and keepeth not his commandments, is a liar, and the truth is not in him." This world, with Satan at the helm, is sailing daily into lies and false truths, fooling many, even the sophisticated and the elite.

In 2 Cor 4:4, it states, "In whom the god of this world hath blinded the minds of them which believe not, lest the light of the glorious gospel of Christ, who is the image of God, should shine unto them." And 2 Cor 4:6 says, "For God, who commanded the light to shine out of darkness, hath shined in our hearts, to give the light of the knowledge of the glory of God in the face of Jesus Christ." Darkness and lies cannot compete with the light or the truth. That's why the enemy does his best to keep people in darkness or in ignorance. He knows if our hearts receive *the truth* he's lost his hold on man. Oh, he will try us, but if we stay in the light or truth, Jesus will not lose one—no, not one of us. But if you leave the light or the truth, you are then in the grasp of the enemy. "If a man abide not in me, he is cast forth as a branch, and is withered; and men gather them, and cast them into the fire, and they are burned" (John 15:6). Without the truth, man must bear the consequences of his fallen nature. The enemy banks on the mindset of ignorance or darkness, hoping that man will die in that truth. Even as I write, my heart is heavy, knowing that real salvation is so close but yet so far for many.

There are so many messages of prosperity throughout the world right now, and I thank God for them, but again, salvation was the message of the Apostles. We have to make sure, as apostles, pastors, evangelists, prophets, and teachers, that the message of true salvation stays in our mouths. When we do revivals or speak for Christ, we can't take for granted that men and women are really in the arms of Christ. I realize that some have been sent to preach the message of prosperity, but we have to remember we are *all* responsible for the salvation message. The blood will be on our hands. "Wherefore I take you to record this day that I am pure from the blood of all men. For I have not shunned to declare unto you all the counsel of God" (Acts 20:26–27). The whole plan or purpose of God is what Paul was stating. He was saying that he told the people everything God wanted them to know; he didn't leave anything out. He was saying, "I didn't take anything for granted. I preached Jesus and nothing else." Paul is literally saying our hearts must be filled and washed with the word, with Jesus.

That is why it is so important that we first deal with our mind, which surrounds the heart. Remember how the mind works. When we think about things in our mind and finally come to a conclusion, it rests in our heart, which is a *holder of truths*. We serve God with our minds. As 1 Chronicles 28:9 says, "And thou, Solomon my son, know thou the God of thy father, and serve him with a perfect heart and with a willing mind: for the LORD searcheth all hearts, and understandeth all the imaginations of the thoughts: if thou seek him, he will be found of thee; but if thou forsake him, he will cast thee off forever."

So if this is true, we need to be very careful what we think about, right? Right. Jesus says through Paul, in Philippians 4:8, "Finally, brethren, whatsoever things are true, whatsoever things are honest, whatsoever things are just, whatsoever things are pure, whatsoever things are lovely, whatsoever things are of good report; if there be any virtue, and if there be any praise, think on these things. Because if you think on these things eventually you will believe them to be true, and when you do your heart shall be filled." So, the enemy works day and night on what you think about. He realizes if he can conquer your thoughts, he will have access to your heart.

In the Old Testament, in the book of Proverbs 23:7, it says, "For as he thinketh in his heart, so is he: Eat and drink, saith he to thee; but his heart is not with thee." The Greek word for *thinketh* also means "gatekeeper." A gatekeeper really runs everything. For instance, say one day you want to contact Bill Gates, and when you call, someone answers and it's not Bill but a gatekeeper. Whether you get to Bill or not depends on how he or she is feeling or what the polices are. That's why many in sales would romance the gatekeepers with gifts to find a path to the general manager. This analogy is the same with the spiritual heart. Our mind is the gatekeeper, and whatever you allow in you will eventually be subject to believe, and you will become what you believe. I used to preach a message and I would use the analogy of explaining that your heart is like your room with a door. Whenever the door opens, stuff can come in. Then the door shuts, or the gatekeeper closes. Whatever came in, you shall become. Have you ever wondered why you would be having a blessed day and someone would call or come by and put something in your spirit and would mess your whole day up? It's because the enemy wants the heart. Jesus speaks about the guarding of your heart in Proverbs 4:23: "Keep thy heart with all diligence; for out of it are the issues of life." Watch over your heart because it is the most cherished spiritual member that you have.

The enemy normally conquers the heart through our ignorance, thus luring us into thoughts we shouldn't be having in the first place. He hopes that just some of this stuff sticks or falls into the heart. Paul states it clearly: "Lest Satan should get an advantage of us: for we are not ignorant of his devices" (2 Cor 2:11). Knowledge is the key. Remember, Jesus is the light, and he issues knowledge, but Satan is darkness, and he deals with ignorance. "My people are destroyed for lack of knowledge: because thou hast rejected knowledge, I will also reject thee"

(Hosea 4:6). The heart holds truths, so the heart hungers for truth and the heart desperately need and seek truth. We have to satisfy this hunger for our hearts, not with junk food, but with a well-balance diet of the word of God. This truth enlightens people about their destiny.

There is a scripture that I really love and I am extremely intrigued by it. "Where there is no vision, the people perish: but he that keepeth the law, happy is he" (Proverbs 29:18). This scripture is saying people who do not have a vision or purpose from God will do anything in life. The Hebrew word for *perish* also means "no restraint." These people have no restraint from sin. I will give an example: you have this young boy who wanted to be a doctor. He bought a black doctor's bag at the age of twelve saving soda bottles. He put his nose to the grindstone, studying and reading every medical book he could find. One day, one of his friends asked him to ride with them, but he knew they were known for destroying property with childish pranks. He thought about it, and when he was preparing to go, his mom said, "Be careful and don't forget about your future." The young man stopped in his tracks and thought. When the guys showed up, he told them he was busy. Why would he change his mind? The vision of the future, of his life, gave him the restraint to deny mischief. It's the same way for the man or woman of God. Some stuff we just cannot do; our destiny is too great. We just can't live immorally. Our futures are banking on restraint, because the best is yet to come, I promise.

So with vision and the truth of God, we can't go wrong. Vision is a clip of what God is going to do. God will show us clips of the finished work of our success. He does not show us the beginning or the preparation for success. The reason he don't show us the struggles and pains of making it to the palace is because we may say, "God, use someone else. I'm just fine here." Remember Joseph in Genesis. God showed him a dream of him being in a palace, and his brothers were bowing down to him. But did you notice God didn't show him that pit or him being sold as a slave, and he surely didn't show him being throw into prison. If so, Joseph might have said, "God, my brother Rueben would be a better prince." But God's vision brings instruction, and we cannot go wrong. Truth is even important to the very vision God gives.

Satan uses subliminal messages in every instance. He realizes what truth does to the heart of man. He knows truth but extinguishes it. Satan knows truth but rebels against it. The scripture in James states that even demons believe, but they rebel against God. Believing that God exists is not enough. You must obey him if he is your Lord. Demons can never have Jesus as Lord, even though they know he is Lord.

The enemy once was with the Lamb of God. He once worshiped the father and the son. Ezekiel 28:17–18 states, "Thine heart was lifted up because of thy beauty, thou hast corrupted thy wisdom by reason of thy brightness: I will cast thee to the ground, I will lay thee before kings, that they may behold thee. Thou hast defiled thy sanctuaries by the multitude of thine iniquities, by the iniquity of thy traffick; therefore will I bring forth a fire from the midst of thee, it shall devour thee, and I will bring thee to ashes upon the earth in the sight of all them that behold thee." So he knows what it takes to please God but denies the power of God. He denies God because he wants the throne of God, which he can never have. So he quests to have his kingdom here on earth, to deceive everyone he can to gain this kingdom. He wants his kingdom to be as great as God's. So it's really all about pride and prestige. Sounds familiar, doesn't it? Look at the world as we know it. Everyone is seeking power, prestige, and a certain type of status. It is simply the foot print of Satan himself. This foe is a definite enemy to the heart of man.

Often, the enemy brings storm after storm, simply to upset us so we might quit servicing God. That's his plan. Silly, isn't it? But that's his plan for the saved. For the unbelievers, he seeks to never let you know the love of God. What is the Love of God? The truth. Let me give you a small nugget of wisdom here. Whenever the enemy attacks, I mean really attacks, you need to stop and think about what you were about to do. I tell churches all around the country that when he comes in like a flood, God will lift a standard: Jesus, the truth. But at that moment, stop and ask yourself, "What was I preparing to do?" The reason I say this is because God gave me a revelation about how, when you start to get close to the father or too close to a miracle, Satan attacks, hoping to distract you. He's keen on distraction. John 10:10: "The thief cometh not, but for to steal, and to kill, and to destroy: I am come that they might have life, and that they might have it more abundantly." Here, Jesus tells us that the devil is here to steal and kill and destroy. How? The devil does it by distorting the truth. Again, Satan is the father of lies. It's his native tongue, his language. Easton states in his dictionary, "He is the constant enemy of God, of Christ, of the divine kingdom, of the followers of Christ, and of all truth; full of falsehood and all malice, and exciting and seducing to evil in every possible way." He knows if he gets the heart, the body will follow. Remember my friend from earlier. When the truth entered his heart through commentaries and even influence from celebrities, then he agreed and he started changing. He concluded that what he heard was true. This is the heart of man and woman. Remember, when he comes in like a flood, stop and think, "What was I going to do before the attack?" or "What was I thinking?"

Chapter 6
You

In the book of James, he speaks of three enemies of man: first, the world; second, Satan; and third, you. In this chapter we will talk about you. That's right, we can be our worst enemy. In Deuteronomy 29:19, the Lord states, "And it come to pass, when he heareth the words of this curse, that he bless himself in his heart, saying, I shall have peace, though I walk in the imagination of mine heart, to add drunkenness to thirst."

When we become our worst enemy is when we accept our own truth. I believe one of the worst truths that we place in our hearts is simply, "God understands." When we place that truth in our hearts, our body will soon follow. What if you put the scripture John 8:51 in your heart? "Verily, verily, I say unto you, If a man keep my saying, he shall never see death, in our heart, as the truth." What would happen to our body? The word *death* here means "second death." Now if we believe this to be the truth, our body will follow. *The body is a slave to the heart.* The heart is not a slave to the body.

I can remember a well-known man of God who preached a message of *stinking thinking.* That phrase is so significant because this is where man falls so often, simply by his own silly thinking.

When we try to bring God down to man's thinking and man's ways, it is just simply a fallacy. Let's look at scripture. "These things hast thou done, and I kept silence; thou thoughtest that I was altogether such an one as thyself: but I will reprove thee, and set them in order before thine eyes" (Psalm 50:21). In this scripture, man thought because God did not punish him immediately, and instead was silent, God was like man. Man makes promises all the time and does not follow through, but God is not like man. "God's thoughts are not your thoughts, neither are your ways my ways, saith the LORD. For as the heavens are higher than the earth, so are my ways higher than your ways, and my thoughts than your thoughts" (Isaiah 55:8–9). But man always tries to equate God's ways to man; that is the first problem that has to be mastered, and it starts with us. We have to understand this before we can fight the ways of the world or the enemy himself.

God is not a man. He doesn't think like man, he doesn't behave like man, and he will not compromise like man. He is God and God alone. He will not change to our ways, but we must change to his. When we can comprehend this, we can grow closer to a holy God. He's waiting patiently for you. Learn about him through Jesus, and watch your relationship and intimacy explode in Christ. He's a great God. God's based his whole existence on his truth, his word. I use to preach a message called "He's God because He'll Do What He Said He'll Do." No other entity can do exactly what it says. The sun doesn't set at the same time each day. The greatest king doesn't do everything he says he can do. But God, he can do what he says. "God is not a man, that he should lie; neither the son of man, that he should repent: hath he said, and shall he not do it? or hath he spoken, and shall he not make it good?" (Numbers 23:19). He is God, and there is no one like him.

So we should not fool ourselves with false truths or old fables about our father. We must grow to know him. Remember, scripture says that if we don't keep his word, we don't know him. And if we say we know him and don't keep his word, scripture says we are a liar and *the truth* is not in us (1 John 2:4).

As I write, I feel someone is saying, "It can't be that easy. If I just study the truth, which is Jesus, I will start to do better." Well, it is that easy. Matthew 11:28–30 says, "Come unto me, all ye that labour and are heavy laden, and I will give you rest. Take my yoke upon you, and learn of me; for I am meek and lowly in heart: and ye shall find rest unto your souls. For my yoke is easy, and my burden is light." See, it is really that easy. Only Jesus can change a heart. You heard this many times but really didn't know what it meant. Now you do. *Change the heart and change the person.*

Paul states in the word that he is a bondservant to Christ, and that should be our declaration, also. We don't belong to ourselves any longer. We have been bought with a price. As 1 Cor 6:19–20 says, "What? know ye not that your body is the temple of the Holy Ghost which is in you, which ye have of God, and ye are not your own? For ye are bought with a price: therefore glorify God in your body, and in your spirit, which are God's." One thing that I love about my relationship with Jesus is that it is Christ's. What do I mean? If I place his truth in my heart, then it's up to Christ, not me, to produce. Some seasoned saints have not yet figured this out. It's that simple: give it to Jesus and watch him work through you. Man's biggest problem is that he still wants to own himself. I once used that analogy in a message.

What if, for example, Hertz, the car rental company, purchased a fleet of HHR's and marked and stamped them accordingly. Then Hertz let a customer rent the vehicle, and the customer stopped and went inside a 7-11. While in the store, the rented car decided to take off and let a racecar driver drive him on the track. Now of course a car cannot do such a thing, but if it could, would it be correct? Obviously not. Satan does the same thing. Jesus pays the price, and Satan connives until he can take possession and drives us the way he pleases. Satan didn't pay anything and has the audacity to tell Jesus, "Hey, let me drive him. I didn't take the wheel, he gave it freely to me." We belong to Jesus. Ye are not your own. For ye are bought with a price; therefore glorify God in your body, and in your spirit, which are God's.

I once had a member who asked me if tattoos were sinful. I sent him to this scripture: "In ye shall not make any cuttings in your flesh for the dead, nor print any marks upon you: I am the LORD" (Leviticus 19:28). Our bodies are not our own. We do not belong to ourselves, and that is a hard pill to swallow. But the statement is definitely true. And this is one of the main issues man has is being his own enemy.

If we can master the thought of belonging to someone else, we can master the kingdom of God. When we realize that before we were purchased, we were lost, slaves to sin, only then can we even entertain salvation. The natural man has to realize that he is bound and not free. This is hard to imagine, because as it stands, he can go where he desires. This seems like freedom, but when he really looks at his habits of sin or flesh, he will find that he is a slave of the ways of the kingdom of Satan. In Romans 7:4–7, it says, "Wherefore, my brethren, ye also are become dead to the law by the body of Christ; that ye should be married to another, even to him who is raised from the dead, that we should bring forth fruit unto God. For when we were in the flesh, the motions of sins, which were by the law, did work in our members to bring forth fruit unto death. But now we are delivered from the law, that being dead wherein we were held; that we should serve in newness of spirit, and not in the oldness of the letter. What shall we say then? Is the law sin? God forbid. Nay, I had not known sin, but by the law: for I had not known lust, except the law had said, 'Thou shalt not covet.'"

So when man realizes he's not free, then and only then can he seek a true liberator, Jesus. Let me give a little story of slavery. I knew a young man who was not saved, and I knew it plainly. I wanted him in the kingdom very badly. As we drove down the highway one day, I started to talk to him about God, to no avail. So the Lord gave me a question to ask him, and it went as follows. "Are you a slave?"

This young black man, as you can imagine, looked at me as if I had insulted him in the worst way. He answered, "No, I'm not a slave and can go where I want, when I want."

Now I knew his girlfriend, and she was a beautiful young lady. So I asked him, "Can you stop having sex with your girlfriend when you want?" not knowing that they were having sex but knowing what society accepts now.

He said, "So this is what it's about."

I said, "No, but can you stop for six weeks?"

He said, "Sure I can." So we got on another subject, and when he was getting out of the car, I reminded him about the six weeks, and he said, "Watch me."

So, two weeks passed, and then three weeks, and then I got a call. I answered and asked who was calling, and the young man said, "This is Kunta Kinte." He realized that he was a slave to the kingdom of Satan. If a person can honestly say that he is a slave, then he has a chance at receiving the loving hand of Jesus.

Self truths are interchangeable with the first two enemies, the world and Satan. Yet there are some distinctive differences when it comes to man himself. Galatians 6:3 states, "For if a man think himself to be something, when he is nothing, he deceiveth himself." There is that word *think*. Remember the gatekeeper. Proverbs 23:7 says, "For as he thinketh in his heart, so is he." One of the biggest problems in the church is pride. We let this false truth into our hearts, which brings destruction. This truth is running like wildfire, not only in the world but in the church. This truth causes separations, divorces, and astronomical confusion. James 3:16 says, "For where envying and strife is, there is confusion and every evil work." All this comes from thinking too much of ourselves. God even says to let others lift you up. You don't have to do this yourself. Your gifts from God will make room for you, even in the presence of kings. That is *the* truth, not *a* truth. But pride lurks through the corridors of hearts, causing problems not only among families but also in public.

I spoke about this once. Have you ever seen someone who was extremely talented, but his contentious attitude washed out the talent? That is the way it is in the kingdom of God. Many are anointed to do great things for God, like singing, preaching, and teaching. The word *anoint* means to rub in, and that is exactly what the Holy Spirit does to his children. Exodus 31:3 states, "I have filled him with the Spirit of God, with skill, ability, and knowledge." The anointing of God gives you the skill, ability, and knowledge to do the things God has called you to do. So quit saying, "I can't do it." If God calls you to it, you have the power to do it, so stay the course. But in some people who are anointed, you see that thing that you know doesn't belong, that prideful character. There is a difference between confidence in Christ and pride. Being confident in Christ is being assured in him and not ourselves. For example, I'm more than a conqueror. God has made me more than a conqueror through his son, Jesus. But some walk in their own ability and always lift themselves up. They will not wait until others see that goodness that only God can give. These issues are based on the truths they have in their hearts.

The apostles wrote about battling with self-imposed afflictions. Often, in our mess we've blamed Satan. I remember years ago, an old elder used to tell a story you've probably heard. It was about Satan sitting on the porch of the church with his chin in his hand, shaking his head. Then a stranger walked by and said, "What's wrong, man?"

Satan stated, "They're in there lying about me again." I like this story because sometimes it's really us and not so much the devil. The devil only has the power that we let him have. He presses to implant his truth in our hearts. If you kill the lie, you kill the devil.

Moreover, men compromise truth, and to justify it, they enter territories that the enemy occupies. Thus, failure comes as surely as morning.

So far, we've talked about three enemies that seek to win the heart: the world, Satan, and you. Now let's talk about the fourth entity that seeks the heart of man.

Chapter 7
Jesus, the Truth

All God ever wanted from man was to be in his presence. I know that sounds strange to some, but he longs for the presence of man. Not that he needs man, but he loves man. In Genesis 1:26, God said, "Let us make man in our image, after our likeness: and let them have dominion over the fish of the sea, and over the fowl of the air, and over the cattle, and over all the earth, and over every creeping thing that creepeth upon the earth." All God ever wanted was fellowship with man. He even created us in resemblance of himself. I tell people the biggest reason Satan hates believers and even unbelievers is because we look like God, and that just angers him. I've heard it said before that the devil won't bother unbelievers, but I beg to differ. Even the unbeliever still resembles God. *But when Christ comes into the unbeliever's life, then he not only resembles God, now he acts like God.* Again, all God ever wanted was for man to be in his presence.

All Adam and Eve had to do was love God and to oversee a beautiful place called Eden. There was no sickness, no hunger, and everything you needed was there. But man broke fellowship with God by sinning against God. This sin wasn't stealing, smoking, or adultery. Most people think these are the most hideous sins.

But the sin was rebellion. I know rebellion is the cause of many falling away from God. Because of this fall, Adam and Eve were escorted out of this paradise. God wanted the world to see what *God and man could do together*. I think this is a nugget of wisdom; God and man work together. God banks on man to accomplish his will. Some labor with this because they think God will do something even if man doesn't carry out his will. But I conclude that there will always be someone, somewhere to carry out God's will. And guess what? God knows this. I tell people, "Even though you're not praying, I promise you someone's praying somewhere in the earth realm every moment." I thank God for that in these perilous times.

After the departure, man's heart became bitter, troubled, and evil. Genesis 6:5 says, "And GOD saw that the wickedness of man was great in the earth, and that every imagination of the thoughts of his heart was only evil continually. God even repented that he made man." Genesis 6:7–8 states, "And the LORD said, I will destroy man whom I have created from the face of the earth; both man, and beast, and the creeping thing, and the fowls of the air; for it repenteth me that I have made them. But God showed mercy and grace even through the dark hearts of man. But Noah found grace in the eyes of the LORD."

In everything man did, God still sought to bring man back to fellowship. But God knew the only way he could bring man back was to change the heart of man. He knew that with man not being in his presence, the heart of man had no chance. So God called people to be his priests and to call man back to him. Exodus 19:5–6 says, "Now therefore, if ye will obey my voice indeed, and keep my covenant, then ye shall be a peculiar (valuable) treasure unto me above all people: for all the earth is mine: And ye shall be unto me a kingdom of priests, and an holy nation. These are the words which thou shalt speak unto the children of Israel." God called these people to him, to sound the horn for man to come back to him. Israel failed.

Then God called some out of Israel to bring Israel back to him, so they could go into the world and bring the world to him. These men were called the Levites. Today, they would be called preachers. And guess what? The Levites sinned or failed, too, with greed and self-indulgence. Then, after the fallible priests, God called prophets to tell the priests to turn back to God, and for the priests to tell the people of Israel to turn back to God, so Israel could go into the world to turn them to God. And guess what happened next? The priests killed the prophets. The prophets were simply trying to tell them what sayeth the Lord.

No one could turn the heart of man, and after all else had failed, God sent himself wrapped in human flesh in the fullness of time. Galatians 4:4–7 says, "But when the fullness of the time was come, God sent forth his Son, made of a woman, made under the law, to redeem them that were under the law, that we might receive the adoption of sons. And because ye are sons, God hath sent forth the Spirit of his Son into your hearts, crying, 'Abba, Father, wherefore thou art no more a servant, but a son; and if a son, then an heir of God through Christ.'" After God tried man after man after man, then he sent his only begotten son to *change the heart of man.*

The law could not change the heart of man, but it showed man his heart as a mirror shows a reflection of the face. The Pharisees tried to use the law not only as a mirror but they thought the law could clean them. Never has a mirror cleaned our face after it showed a flaw. Romans 8:3–5 states, "For what the law could not do, in that it was weak through the flesh, God sending his own Son in the likeness of sinful flesh, and for sin, condemned sin in the flesh: That the righteousness of the law might be fulfilled in us, who walk not after the flesh, but after the Spirit. For they that are after the flesh do mind the things of the flesh; but they that are after the Spirit the things of the Spirit."

God knew the three enemies would chase down and pursue the heart of man with desperate energy. The heart of man cannot stand against such persistent foes alone. So Jesus started his ministry and changed hearts from countryside to countryside. How, you may ask? Well, remember, Jesus is the truth. John 14:6 says, "Jesus saith unto him, I am the way, the truth, and the life: no man cometh unto the Father, but by me." So for Jesus to change their hearts, they had to *believe* what he said. Remember, when you believe something to be truth, it sits in your heart, and your body or works follow the heart accordingly.

As you can see, for truth to be evident, there must be belief.

Chapter 8
Paul's Works vs. Jesus' works

Let's talk about the works of man. The Greek word for *work* (*sergon* er·gon) means "an act, a deed, a thing done." What is Paul saying in Ephesians 2:8–9? "By grace are ye saved through faith; and that not of yourselves: it is the gift of God: Not of works, lest any man should boast." And what is Jesus saying about works? In Revelation 22:12, he says, "And, behold, I come quickly; and my reward is with me, to give every man according as his work shall be." Now for years when I was growing up, I would hear the preacher say salvation has nothing to do with works. I can remember someone would ask him about Jesus' teaching in the New Testament, and he couldn't really convey his answer to the parishioners. After his explanations, they would still ask the question, "Why is Paul contradicting Jesus?" But I will try to explain this because I believe it is of paramount importance for the kingdom of God. I will clarify that what Paul was saying was exactly what Jesus was saying.

So first, let's examine Paul's teachings, starting with Ephesians chapter 2. Paul starts by writing about times past: how we walked in the flesh or the truths of the flesh or the truths of the world or the truths of Satan. In verse two, he discusses the *spirit* that *worketh* (literally, to work for one, aid one) in the children of disobedience. Notice *spirit* with a lowercase "s" and the word *worketh*. First, *spirit* here is not the Spirit of God, but the spirit of Satan, the father of lies or false truths. The false truths *worketh* in the children of disobedience. Where are these truths setting? They are setting in the heart of man. So in times past, you walked in false truths. Let's go a little deeper. What false truths? Remember a few chapters back. The world's truths, the devil's truths, and your own truths all worketh in us. Works are a normal factor that comes from the heart. Works are not bad in general. But the end time church is troubled by this word. They are so afraid of someone screaming *legalism* that many miss what Jesus was trying to say. Every one of us is producing works every day. We might as well accept it; it's just a fact of life. When we labor in college, we are not attending just to be in college; we are seeking the rewards of our works. So works are a part of all our lives. Even infants produce works. When infants want milk, they scream until we can't handle it anymore and give in to the scream, wake up out of a deep sleep, and give the bottle to them. Then they quiet down. The crying are their works, and they get the reward the milk. The question is, what type of works will you produce? It's all based on the truths in the heart.

When we were lost, there was no chance of changing our own hearts. God, by his mercy, sent his grace (strength) to bring the son where we could receive him. Then grace gives us the strength to receive him. In the believer's Bible commentary, its infers this: grace is how God exerts his holy influence upon souls; turns them to Christ; keeps, strengthens, and increases them in Christian faith, knowledge, affection; and kindles them to exercise Christian virtues.[5] This is definitely unmerited favor. We did nothing; we couldn't change our own hearts, but God's grace allowed the truth to change it. Let's get back to works or I will start praising God right here in this seat.

So grace (God's strength) allowed us, when the truth (Jesus) came, to understand the truth even though it burned our flesh; it went directly against the truths of our carnal heart. So as Paul says, not of works (your personal works, by your strength) but by grace (God's strength), or God works through you. How do we get God's works from us? Simply by God changing our hearts with his truth; our bodies will always perform based on what's in our hearts. *When the truth enters the heart, the repercussion is that our works line up with what is in our hearts, and if the truth is there, our works are like Jesus'.* Thus, whatever truth is in the heart, that is what the body will perform or reproduce. Look at Ephesians 2:10: "For we are his workmanship, created in Christ Jesus unto good works, which God hath before ordained that we should walk in them." So, now you should see Paul's words lining up perfectly with Jesus' teaching. Let's look at Revelation 22:12: "And, behold, I come quickly; and my reward is with me, to give every man according as his work shall be." The Greek word for *reward* literally means "dues paid for work; wages, hire; reward: used of the fruit naturally resulting from toils and endeavors."[6] Jesus teaches here about receiving rewards of works. What works? The answer is the works of the heart. So those who receive high pay or heaven for their work can be confident they had nothing to do with it; they believed and received truth and couldn't have done that if God's grace didn't turn them to believe the truth. So what God gives us starts and ends with him.

However, Satan flips, jumps, screams, and fights to get man not to receive the truth. He fools men into believing that it has nothing to do with works, not allowing men to receive the truth about works. So men live in folly and sin right in the church, and the sinners look on and reject the church and God. But if they really knew God, they would keep his word, which is truth. As 1 John 2:3–4 says, "And hereby we do know that we know him, if we keep his commandments. He that saith, 'I know him,' and keepeth not his commandments, is a liar, and the truth is not in him." No truth, no good works, no truth, no God. Know truth, know good works, know truth, know God. It's all about the truth, Jesus. So works are a necessity, no doubt.

Also when Christ works through us, it fulfills the law. Please keep reading and don't throw the book away now. I know I hit a sacred cow. Let's look at scripture. Romans 8:1–4: "There is therefore now no condemnation to them which are in Christ Jesus, who walk not after the flesh, but after the Spirit. For the law of the Spirit of life in Christ Jesus hath made me free from the law of sin and death." For what the law could not do, in that it was weak through the flesh, God sending his own son in the likeness of sinful flesh, and for sin, condemned sin in the flesh, that the righteousness of the law might be fulfilled in us, who walk not after the flesh, but after the spirit.

Jesus did not come to destroy the law but to fulfill the law through us. That's important. The scripture says "those that are in Christ Jesus." This is important, too. John 15:7 says, "If ye abide in me, and my words abide in you, ye shall ask what ye will, and it shall be done unto you." Jesus is simply saying he is in our hearts. The law was like a mirror to show us sin, but it could not change or clean our faces. But Jesus changes our hearts. Remember the works or the body will follow whatever truth enters our hearts. Rev 22:12 says, "Jesus will give according to the works on that day." Do not be fooled; this is not legalism or self-righteousness. You can't change yourself; only the truth can change a heart and produce good works.

Why can't some receive Jesus Christ in salvation? The answer is simple: pride. As 1 Peter 5:5 says, "For God resisteth the proud, and giveth grace to the humble." Some will not submit themselves to the word, to Jesus. Pride keeps them from receiving truth, that their heart may be changed. I had many ask, "Pastor, why there are so many people on the streets, on crack, and addicted to so many different habits?" The answer is that they will not submit themselves to Jesus but will try to solve their own problems. The truth of the world, Satan, and even ourselves always leads us to answers without Christ. These are good people, but they don't have a chance without the truth of God. They live by their own ability and nurture their views. Some will go to church, and many will not submit completely to the word but will walk in a false humility. Pride always find its way back. Pride stops the grace of God or the strength of God from fostering them. As 1 Peter 5:5 states, "God gives grace (strength) to the humble (In the Greek, humble means not rising far from the ground), but resist (refuses to give strength) the proud." Why would we need his strength? Remember, grace is how God exerts his holy influence upon souls; turns them to Christ; keeps, strengthens, and increases them in Christian faith, knowledge, affection; and kindles them to exercise Christian virtues.[7] Without his strength or grace, we could not even turn to Jesus.

The devil, wants us to believe a lie is the truth. That's why the idea that God understands is not *the* truth, but *a* truth. When we are in sin, all God understands is that *we don't know him in that area.* As 1 John 2:3–4 states, "And hereby we do know that we know him, if we keep his commandments. He that saith, 'I know him,' and keepeth not his commandments, is a liar, and the truth is not in him." When we sin, we do not know God, and it is of paramount importance that we learn about him. How? First, we must find the truth about that circumstance or what God has said about it. Then we must accept that as the truth. Then we must believe it, and when we do, it will become truth as we know it and falls into our heart, and the body will have no choice but to follow.

As 1 Peter 5:5 says, "Yea, all of you be subject one to another, and be clothed with humility: for God resisteth the proud, and giveth grace to the humble." Grace is a spirit, and so are we. Grace is not only unmerited favor; grace is God's' strength. As 2 Cor 12:9 states, "And he said unto me, 'My grace is sufficient for thee: for my strength is made perfect in weakness.'" God said in 1 Peter 5:5 that he resists the proud but gives his strength or grace to the humble. The reason prideful people sin time after time, even when they try to walk in the way of God, is because they do not have grace giving them the power to walk it out. Prideful people will not submit themselves to the word of God. Remember, whatever you believe as truth, especially the word of God, will sit in your heart, and your body or works will follow.

When God invites us to the kingdom, he strips away all the things that made us who we are, sheet by sheet, until nothing but the original is left. That's what God wanted the entire time. Many of us have no idea who we really are because the world, Satan, and even stuff we have stacked on us, thus making us something we are not. The problem with this is when God starts stripping, it hurts, it embarrasses, it contradicts, it literally brings us to the place where we ask, "Who am I?" This is what God wants.

He can show us who we are through his son, Jesus, the truth. Matthew 19:21–24 says, "Then said Jesus unto his disciples, 'Verily I say unto you, That a rich man shall hardly enter into the kingdom of heaven. And again I say unto you, It is easier for a camel to go through the eye of a needle, than for a rich man to enter into the kingdom of God.'" In this scripture, Jesus tells us that a rich man can hardly enter the kingdom of heaven. We try to envision a man squeezing through the eye of a needle, which would be impossible. But a lot of great men of God were rich, including Solomon and Abraham. So does this mean that they didn't make it into the kingdom of heaven? Surely not. But there was an opening in the wall around a castlelike structure, and this small opening was called the eye of the needle. This opening was so small that a camel could not enter it unless they placed the camel on his knees and they unloaded the supplies from the camel's back. Then they could drag the camel in. Now this wall would surround the castle completely. The wall had two openings: one in the front, which was a huge gate that was guarded with soldiers 24/7; and the second, which was the eye of the needle, which had no guards after a certain time at night. Now if a person with a single camel with supplies wanted to get into the kingdom, they would simply go through the eye of the needle, because it was closer than the main gate. They would have to unload the camel and place him on his knees and drag him through. Now, one camel wouldn't be too much of a chore. But if you were rich and had five hundred camels, then the story changed. No rich man with sense would unload five hundred camels one at a time and drag them one at a time through the eye of the needle. Instead, they would travel around the wall or city, which was very time consuming. But still, it would be time saved compared to unloading and loading. Now how does this help us with Jesus' sayings? Jesus was simply saying that rich men didn't want to unload to get in the kingdom. And *unloading* is the term of importance in this story. Everyone wants the kingdom, but everyone wants to take everything in with them, and Jesus says we should unload. The choice he gives them is him or the stuff. Remember, Jesus told the rich man, "Give everything to the poor and follow me." The man turned away and left with his head lowered. Why did he leave? He chose stuff over Jesus. The man didn't even grasp the scriptures about sowing and receiving a harvest for what you've sown. He didn't even trust Jesus that the word about sowing is true. This is a word in itself.

Chapter 9
Take It from the Heart

The truth must be placed in the heart of man; thus, he shall perish. Many say, "Well, when I get the truth in my heart, all my troubles will be over." I answer with an unequivocal no. There are all types of snares set to entangle the new and old believer. Matthew 13:19 says, "When any one heareth the word of the kingdom, and understandeth it not, then cometh the wicked one, and catcheth away that which was sown in his heart." This is he which received seed by the wayside." Here, the devil preys on emotionalism in the church. His prayer is that we get caught up in the feeling that our heart will go lacking. I used to hear a great bishop from Center Texas say Christians come to church with their head off but go to work wearing it. Simply put, many Christians don't come to church seeking how to learn to know God but come to get their church on. As 1 John 2:4 says, "He that saith, 'I know him,' and keepeth not his commandments, is a liar, and the truth is not in him." However, concerning their jobs many seek how to learn new software to be more valuable and eligible for promotions. They place more value on a resource than on the source. The enemy prays we become confused by the truth or the word, not understanding the way of Christ. Jesus says in

Matthew. 13:19 that the devil will *catcheth away*. Catcheth away what? The truth of God, Jesus Christ, the word. This truth will be sown in the hearts of thousands each Sunday, and at Bible studies, also, only to be caught and removed from the hearts of man. So how do we keep the word or truth in our hearts? Only by understanding the word; *you have to understand it to believe it*. We have to put our heads on when we come to church. By exercising these practices, we are in God's sight, submitting ourselves to him, his word, his son, Jesus. When we understand the word, the enemy has to try to make us believe what God said is a lie. Thus, we would stop seeking him and stop putting effort in understanding his truth.

In Matthew 13:20–21, it states that Jesus tells us how the word or truth brings persecution. "But he that received the seed into stony places, the same is he that heareth the word, and anon with joy receiveth it; yet hath he not root in himself, but dureth for a while: for when tribulation or persecution ariseth because of the word, by and by he is offended." Many times when some show interest in the truth or the word, others, even their family members, will come against them. They might say, "Oh, that old church is no good. Oh that preacher is eerie. You're not going to be one of those old holy rollers, are you?" Or maybe as soon as you hear a great word about prosperity, then that Monday the electric company shuts off your electricity. You normally had two more weeks before cut off, but not this time. Subconsciously, you start leaning back to what was familiar: *a* truth, not *the* truth. But if you had really understood the truth or the word, you would have been waiting for the devil to come lurking as a thief and murderer. But a seed sown on good ground produces a thirty, sixty, or even one-hundred-fold return. The one who believes Jesus' word and understands it will receive and understand even more.[8]

The devil, as I stated before, bombards the heart with false truths. Demons carry this task out. The demons bring thoughts and truths that will cling to the heart of man to change behaviors. But God cleans with his word. John 15:3 says, "Now ye are clean through the word which I have spoken unto you." God's word cleans the heart. Sometimes a heart can be cleaned by someone praying for you, but that person who just had his heart cleaned or had the devil cast out of his heart should immediately get in a Bible-based church, because as John 15:3 says, "Ye are clean through the word which I have spoken unto you." I'll give an example. Jesus talks about this in reference to a man who had been delivered of a demon. The man tried to fill up his home (heart) with traditions and not the truth (Jesus), and the demon came back. Let's just look at scripture. Matthew 12:44–45: "Then he saith, 'I will return into my house from whence I came out'; and when he is come, he findeth it empty, swept, and garnished. Then goeth he, and taketh with himself seven other spirits more wicked than himself, and they enter in and dwell there: and the last state of that man is worse than the first." This man's heart was worse shape at the end than it was initially. When a heart becomes empty because spirits or false truths are cast out a person, the person must immediately get into a Bible-based church. Thus the truth can be preached and taught in a way this person can understand and have his heart filled with the truth, Jesus.

Chapter 10
Obedience

It has long been said that obedience is better than sacrifice. There is one statement that I always say: there is just one thing God don't have; he has everything else. He has our possessions, our family, and even our beauty. But there is one thing we don't have to give him. He longs for it dearly, but we can fight against giving it, and many take it to their graves. If you haven't already guessed, that thing is our obedience. Why is obedience so important to God? It means everything to him. He even equates it to your love for him. In John 14:21. Jesus states, "He that hath my commandments, and keepeth them, he it is that loveth me: and he that loveth me shall be loved of my Father, and I will love him, and will manifest myself to him."

Obedience plays an important role in our salvation. Revelation 22:12 says, "And, behold, I come quickly; and my reward is with me, to give every man according as his work shall be." The Greek word for *reward* also means "dues paid for work; wages, hire; reward" Our obedience produces a reward. So how do we show this type of obedience? By letting Jesus enter our hearts; this will produce good works. Thus, we shall receive a good reward from Jesus.

There is even a direct correlation between obedience and the receiving of the Holy Ghost. Let's look at scripture. Acts 5:32: "And we are his witnesses of these things; and so is also the Holy Ghost, whom God hath given to them that obey him." Remember earlier when I said *obey* and *believe* are used somewhat synonymously in scripture. Here is a good example: if you believe God or obey God, you shall receive the Holy Ghost. You cannot biblically believe something and not obey it, or obey something willfully and not believe it. So, when you obey (believe) the truth (Jesus), you shall receive the Holy Ghost. That should be encouraging to you if you wonder sometimes if you have the Holy Ghost. Relax; now you know how to get him.

God states in 1 Samuel 15:22–23, "And Samuel said, 'Hath the LORD as great delight in burnt offerings and sacrifices, as in obeying the voice of the LORD?' Behold, to obey is better than sacrifice, and to hearken than the fat of rams. For rebellion is as the sin of witchcraft, and stubbornness is as iniquity and idolatry. Because thou hast rejected the word of the LORD, he hath also rejected thee from being king." God wishes for his children to obey him. Why? Because God knows what's best for us. He created us, he knows what makes us tick, he knows what our demise will be. King Saul used every excuse to disobey God, but God states that rebellion is as the sin of witchcraft. People don't understand witchcraft. They think it has something to do with brooms and spells. But it has to do with going against the truth, against Jesus, with outright rebellion. I believe this is the biggest problem in the kingdom of God now: rebellion. Sons and daughters in the ministry are rebelling against the very ones who tarried with them as their spiritual fathers when others didn't see the promise of God in them. Satan has sown the seed of rebellion.

Matthew 13:39 says, "The enemy that sowed them is the devil"; he sown some to effect the sons and daughters to rebel against their fathers.

How does the enemy fight obedience with truth? He tries to compromise the truth. Let's look at how even Satan tries Jesus and how Jesus handles it. Matthew 4:2–11 says, "And when he had fasted forty days and forty nights, he was afterward an hungred. And when the tempter came to him, he said, 'If thou be the Son of God, command that these stones be made bread.' But he answered and said, 'It is written, Man shall not live by bread alone, but by every word that proceedeth out of the mouth of God.' Then the devil taketh him up into the holy city, and setteth him on a pinnacle of the temple, And saith unto him, 'If thou be the Son of God, cast thyself down: for it is written, He shall give his angels charge concerning thee: and in their hands they shall bear thee up, lest at any time thou dash thy foot against a stone.' Jesus said unto him, 'It is written again, Thou shalt not tempt the Lord thy God.' Again, the devil taketh him up into an exceeding high mountain, and sheweth him all the kingdoms of the world, and the glory of them; And saith unto him, 'All these things will I give thee, if thou wilt fall down and worship me.' Then saith Jesus unto him, 'Get thee hence, Satan: for it is written, Thou shalt worship the Lord thy God, and him only shalt thou serve.' Then the devil leaveth him, and, behold, angels came and ministered unto him."

Jesus uses the truth on Satan, and he leaves. The devil even tries to use false truths on Jesus. In Matthew 4:6, it states, "If thou be the Son of God, cast thyself down: for it is written, He shall give his angels charge concerning thee: and in their hands they shall bear thee up, lest at any time thou dash thy foot against a stone." Satan takes God's truth out of context to try to get Jesus to commit suicide. The enemy will use the truth out of context to get man to rebel against God.

This whole book is based on the truth of God. Certainly, because of the lack of the truth, our nation has turned to chaos. In Galatians 5:22–23, it states, "But the fruit of the Spirit is love, joy, peace, longsuffering, gentleness, goodness, faith, meekness, temperance: against such there is no law." When we connect ourselves to the Spirit, we connect ourselves to the truth. Have you ever looked back in the past to the fifties and sixties? I remember not too long ago, a lost scene of *Leave It to Beaver* was recovered. The reason it was never used is because it had a commode in it. They could not run it because the television audience was not ready for a commode. We have come a long way from screening out commodes to allowing heaven only knows. What happened? Did we grow wiser with real truth? Or did we leave truth?

We are seeing where two out of every five black teenagers end up in prison. We are watching governors caught up in sex scandals and preachers falling like flies to the snares of the enemy. What happened? Some of the biggest investors in the twenty-first century will be investing in security and prisons. Yes, billions will be made in providing security and prisons for our society. What happened? Let's look at Gal 5:22–23. God tells us that the fruit of the spirit not fruits, but fruit is love, joy, peace … Against such there is **no law**. When people receive Jesus, the Spirit of God, all those attributes are in them. When people are carrying these attributes, no law is needed. When there are morals, no law or sheriff is needed. When there is no Spirit, there are false truths and lies. When people live their lives based on lies, they produce immorality. When our hearts are filled with lies and false truths, our bodies produce works accordingly. The fruit that will be produced is pain and anguish.

So, what can we do? For starters, we can put prayer back in the schools. We can place biblical materials back in schools and colleges as requirements. We can train our children in the way of God, and even if they leave for a season, they will know the way back. In the Old Testament days, parents would place necklaces with the commandments of God on their children, so they would not forget them. Or we can do the easy thing: nothing. Some will say, "Well, you know you infringing on others' rights." A. W. Tozer wrote a book called *Born at Midnight*. In the book, he discussed a state of emergency. The inference was that whenever there is a natural disaster in a state or country, all officials, statesman, and anyone with any authority will immediately send out people to save as many lives as possible. In a matter of hours, people, sometimes from all over the world, send food, water, and manpower to help. Everyone responds because of the imminent loss of life. A. W. Tozer states that every day is a state of emergency, because lives are in an imminent danger. Satan is stealing, killing, and ravaging the land, but the church is acting like everything is normal. People are being cast into utter darkness second after second, and we are watching it happen right before our eyes. I come to tell you it's not too late. We don't have to turn this world over to Satan that easily.

Let's look at scripture. Matthew 5:13 says, "Ye are the salt of the earth: but if the salt have lost his savour, wherewith shall it be salted? It is thenceforth good for nothing, but to be cast out, and to be trodden under foot of men." Jesus uses the word *salt* for the Christian. Why salt? In those days, they did not have refrigerators to keep the meat from spoiling. They used salt to preserve food. And as long as the salt has savor, it could preserve the meat. So again, the salt is Christians and the meat in this example is the world. The world is decomposing right before our eyes. But God calls some to be light or salt to stop the decaying of the world, or else all shall be lost. But sometimes the one he calls falls and thus loses his savor. He loses his ability to stop the decay. Jesus says that when we get in this state and stay here, we are thenceforth good for nothing but to be cast out and to be trodden under the feet of men. At that time in Jerusalem, when the salt lost its savor, they would use it as gravel, as we do with pebbles. They would place it on the ground so men could keep their feet clean on rainy days.

Let's look at another word from Jesus. Matthew 5:14–15: "Ye are the light of the world. A city that is set on a hill cannot be hid. Neither do men light a candle, and put it under a bushel, but on a candlestick; and it giveth light unto all that are in the house." Jesus conveys to us that we are the light of this world. A lit city in the New Testament days could be seen even in candle light if on a hill. If we are the light in a dark world, we will accomplish the work of Christ. Believe it or not, there are some people looking for just a flicker of light. The church has to able to produce it. Light not only helps the person who is illuminated; it helps all those around the light, lest they stumble in the dark. We talked earlier about stumbling in the dark. Again, light equates to truth, which leads those who are lost in darkness (lies) to the light or truths of God. Take a look at Matthew 5:16: "Let your light so shine before men, that they may see your good works, and glorify your Father which is in heaven." In this decaying world, Christ doesn't want us to sit back and criticize, but to do something with what he gave us. Remember, the works that you produced in

Jesus, you had nothing to do with them. You believed (obeyed), and Jesus did the rest. You obeyed, and grace touched your heart and your body produced works accordingly. Not only will men see these good works, but the father should be glorified, because these good works will draw men to Jesus.

Chapter 11
Repentance

Now we understand that faith is the belief or conviction in a truth and to believe in anything is to commit to that thing. We know our heart only receives truth as we know it. So we have to make sure only the truth, Jesus, enters our heart. That's why it is paramount importance that we stay in the truth, the word of God. So let's engage in some of God's truth. Numerous times, the Bible speaks about repentance. What is the truth about repentance? The Greek meaning is as follows: a change of mind, as it appears to one who repents of a purpose he has formed or of something he has done.[9] Sometimes man has a way of misunderstanding repentance. In a nutshell, it simply means to turn from a sin or transgression against God and then to turn toward God. The reason this is important is because sometimes we can turn from one thing and turn toward something worse. When we turn toward God, this pleases him. Look at this truth in scripture: "The Lord is not slack concerning his promise, as some men count slackness; but is longsuffering to usward, not willing that any should perish, but that all should come to repentance" (2 Peter 3:9). There is a direct connection between perishing and repentance. When there is no repentance, there is perishing, which here means "second death." The Greek word for *perish* literally means "render useless; to kill; to declare that one must be put to death; to devote or give over to eternal misery in hell; to be lost, ruined, destroyed."[10] Now when you read that verse, what are you changing your mind about or what are you repenting from?

The answer is simple. There are two kingdoms at work on earth. There is the kingdom of Satan or darkness (ignorance). And there is a kingdom of God, which is light (knowledge). God prays that man repent from the ways of the kingdom of Satan. Some believe that when it comes to repenting, it mainly means to repent from illicit sex, or cigarettes, or lying. It does mean those things, but that's not all. It means turning from the way of Satan, the way of the world. This way of the world or Satan will lead to perishing. God's will is that none should perish. Why do you think we need to repent from the world? Because when Jesus came for us, all we had in our hearts was the world. Remember the chapter about how the world affects our truths. God works diligently to capture us with his love (Jesus). It's really a challenge because we are so full of this world and its fleshly ways. But God loves us so much that he continually sends angels, men and women of God, after us with a message of love from heaven. I tell people all the time that there will not be mercy on the day of judgment in a sense. Mercy comes right now—every time you hear a message on the radio or listen to a song about our savior or every time your pastor studies until the late hours just for a word to give you. These are all examples of his loving, compassionate mercy. Every time someone tells you over and over to visit their church, that is mercy. Every time you encounter a near miss at a red light is mercy. Every time your grandmother prayed and explained to you to live a holy life was mercy. Every time sickness came in reference of an irresponsible act, God was trying to give you another chance of mercy. *Repentance.* What an awesome word it is, indeed.

I've heard some say, "I'm going to keep doing it. Why repent? I don't want to be a hypocrite." That is the main trick of the devil. We repent because God says to. When we do that, it means we are submitting to his word. Remember what he said he would do for the humble: give them grace, his strength. Salvation is about obeying. When we obey willingly, that means we really believe. The devil knows this; he once lived with the word, Jesus. So even when you sin, 1 John 1:9 states, if we confess our sins, he is faithful and just to forgive us our sins, and to cleanse us from all unrighteousness. He will forgive them if we repent of them first. Then we can confess our sins, and he will forgive us.

Now you may be thinking that 1 John 1:9 didn't say anything about repenting first. Let me give you an example as I've told many churches. Imagine you have a friend and you just asked him to run to the local Wal-Mart to pick up a clock. How did you ask him? Did you say, "Hey, Fred, would you run to Wal-Mart for me to pick up a clock?" Or would you say, "Fred, would you get up out of that chair and walk over to the table and get your keys and walk toward the door, then open it. Walk through and step down the steps and walk to your car and place the key in door and open the door and sit down." Well, you get the picture. In the days of the New Testament, repentance was as normal as walking. It was a way of life in the kingdom of God. And guess what? It should be now in the kingdom of God.

Now I may shake you here, but read this and continue on. There has never been a sin forgiven that was not repented of.

Never! Before you argue, seek and you will find the truth in scripture. In 1 John 1:9, it states that before you can be forgiven, first you have to confess, and quit the sin. I used to tell a story of a burglar in a bank, stuffing a black bag with one hundred dollars bills. Then the policeman sneaks up on him and says, "Stick 'em up." The burglar continues to stuff the bag, even while the policeman screams, "Stick 'em up."

He pleads with the policeman to forgive him while he's stuffing the bag, shouting, "Please, show me mercy." Now we know the police probably would not show mercy here, but if they were going to, the burglar would first need to stop stuffing the money in the bag. Now I know that seems a little silly to you, but asking for forgiveness while still in the sin is just as silly to God.

"I say unto you, that likewise joy shall be in heaven over one sinner that repenteth, more than over ninety and nine just persons, which need no repentance" (Luke 15:7). God's prayer is that all come or repent to him. Angels jump and Jesus laughs with joy when one sinner turns from the way of the world and turns to the truth of God.

Nowadays, we rarely hear repentance even mentioned in messages over pulpits on Sundays. No wonder some think they just can confess the sin and all is well. Only if you've quit the sin can you confess to a holy God.

Some think that Jesus came so that we can stay in the sin and still be forgiven, but Jesus came to free us from sin. Let's look at the truth: "But God be thanked, that ye were the servants of sin, but ye have obeyed from the heart that form of doctrine which was delivered you. Being then made free from sin, ye became the servants of righteousness" (Romans 6:17–18). Jesus came to free us from the shackles of the world, Satan, and our own shackles.

Jesus came to give us life and help us live more abundantly. Let's look at more truth about this subject: "And now why tarriest thou? Arise, and be baptized, and wash away thy sins, calling on the name of the Lord" (Acts 22:16). What is Jesus speaking about here through his Apostle Paul?

Let's look at a short story. There was once a man in the forest, and he fell down a deep cleft, which resembled a pit. He tried desperately to climb out to no avail. After hours of trying to climb out, he started yelling, "Help! Help, someone!"

Finally, a park ranger showed up and yelled, "Are you all right?"

The man yelled, "No, snakes and wild animals are down here nipping at my heels." He screamed for help again, and the ranger immediately threw down a rope and yelled to the man to tie the rope around him and he would pull him up.

Ten minutes later, the man still screamed for help. The ranger said, "Tie the rope around you," and the man said, "I don't want to do that," and kept screaming.

Eventually, the ranger said, "Just calling for help is not enough. The only way you are going to get out is to tie the rope around you and let me pull you up."

The man said, "I want out but I don't want to do anything." Now we know that if the man really wanted to come out, he would have tied the rope around himself to be lifted out. This story is similar to Paul telling us to call on the name of Jesus to be saved. What does a man do when he's caught up in the ways of the world, bound, tied down, and suffering? He calls on Jesus. But to call you must *believe* Jesus can help you. We have to do something and that is *believe* (commit to). Some call on Jesus but they ignore the rope that he may pull them out.

"Repent ye therefore, and be converted, that your sins may be blotted out, when the times of refreshing shall come from the presence of the Lord" (Acts 3:19). There is a direct correlation between repenting and having your sins blotted out. Here, Peter is conveying the idea of repentance to Israel. Repentance from what? Repenting from religion and the ways of tradition, and turning to Jesus. Jesus is not hung up on rules but on relationships and fellowship. He truly looks at the heart, while men look at the outer body. Repentance is a key word for the kingdom. When we came to Jesus, we brought many sins that needed to be blotted out. Repenting from these things by his strength (grace) allowed us to have them blotted out.

In the Old Testament, intentional sins were never forgiven. Many don't know that. They thought that murders and other hideous crimes could be covered by the blood of animals. "And the priest shall make an atonement for all the congregation of the children of Israel, and it shall be forgiven them; for it is ignorance: and they shall bring their offering, a sacrifice made by fire unto the LORD, and their sin offering before the LORD, for their ignorance" (Numbers 15:25). "Now when these things were thus ordained, the priests went always into the first tabernacle, accomplishing the service of God. But into the second went the high priest alone once every year, not without blood, which he offered for himself, and for the **errors** of the people" (Hebrews 9:6–7). There has never been forgiveness for intentional sin. The blood of goats and calves could not accomplish what only the blood of Jesus could do. "Neither by the blood of goats and calves, but by his own blood he entered in once into the holy place, having obtained eternal redemption for us" (Hebrews 9:12). When Jesus, the high priest, entered the picture, even drug addicts, murderers, prostitutes, and all the others guilty of sins of commission and omission could be forgiven if they repented. Jesus says my burdens are light.

Repentance is about choice. "I call heaven and earth to record this day against you, that I have set before you life and death, blessing and cursing: therefore choose life, that both thou and thy seed may live" (Deuteronomy 30:19). Repentance is tied to life, and staying in sin is tied to death. In that day, if a person unintentionally committed a sin, that person would have to drag an animal to the priest. The priest would prepare the animal, and the person who sinned would have to lay hands on the animal, thus transferring the sin. Sometimes the guilty person would want the priest to kill the animal, but the priest would say, "I didn't sin; you did." The priest would give him the knife, and the guilty party would kill the animal. I tell this story because the only way to atone for a sin is to kill the sacrifice. You may be thinking, "I didn't kill Jesus because I wasn't there two thousand years ago." You're right; you weren't there—but you did kill him. Every time you sinned, you drove a nail into his hands. Every time you transgressed against God, you drove a nail into his feet. Every time you committed iniquities, you stabbed him with a spear. So we all took part in Jesus' crucifixion. We all shared in the responsibility of his pain, his loneliness, and his death. Oh yes, we all did. That was God's plan. How could we claim Jesus as a sacrifice? We had to kill the sacrifice, and we did.

Repentance is tied to obedience, because God is a holy God. God is love, precepts, and principles. He is perfect, he is excellent, and he is our father. God knows sin leads to death. That is why he wants us to come out of it. Satan, on the other hand, is assured that he can keep man in sin by luring him with lust and greed. It is a choice all men must make: the world and Satan, or God.

Chapter 12
Forgiveness

I will spend some time on the subject of forgiveness. This is a truth that is imperative to the kingdom of God. The Hebrew word for *forgiveness* means "send away; a ticket of freedom." To forgive is to send away with debt forgiven. Let's look at forgiveness in the Greek. It means to pardon. Forgiveness is love, and God gives it to whoever repents. That's a promise in his truth. The power of forgiveness is essential in the kingdom of God. Now let us look at forgiveness in the New Testament. The scripture at hand is the basis of forgiveness, and I will explain why. "Take heed to yourselves: If thy brother trespass against thee, rebuke him; and *if he repent*, forgive him. And if he trespass against thee seven times in a day, and seven times in a day turn again to thee, saying, 'I repent'; thou shalt forgive him. And the apostles said unto the Lord, 'Increase our faith'" (Luke 17:3–5). I feel this scripture is the basis of New Testament teachings on forgiveness. Jesus is teaching the apostles about forgiveness. He tells them if your brother (relative, kin, member of the same tribe) trespasses or sins against you, first rebuke him, and *if* he repents, *forgive* him. I figure that one of the apostles asked Jesus, "What if they sin against us more than once? Then what?" And Jesus said if they do it four hundred and ninety times in a twenty-four-hour period and repent four hundred and ninety times, you are to forgive them. The apostles said to Jesus, "Give us *more* faith."

I believe this scripture gives a layout of forgiveness. If someone sins or trespasses against you, the truth tells you to *rebuke* them. Why is that so important? If you rebuke a person, he will normally respond with, "What are you talking about? Yes, I did it. What are you going to do about it?" This is why we must rebuke. Or he may say, "Why are you rebuking me? I did nothing." Let me give a quick example. There once was a man named Jake, and he thought his friend Ben had said something slanderous about him. Jake became furious and bitter. He never said anything to Ben about it. He just held it in. Then one day, Ben was just kidding around, like he always did, about something totally separate from the sore spot that Jake carried. Jake flew off the handle and the friendship was ended. Years passed, and they crossed each other's path at a mall. Out of amazement, they were excited about each other's company. As they conversed, they discussed the quarrel they had. It wasn't long until Ben asked, "Why did you get so uptight that day?"

Jake said, "I had heard you had slandered my name to a guy."

Ben said, "No way. That wasn't me. Glenn did that."

Jake said, "The rumor was it was you, Ben."

Ben said, "No, it was Glenn for sure."

Now if Jake would have rebuked Ben on that day, he would have found out that Ben was innocent. Jesus knew this, and this is just one reason Jesus places rebuking in the process of forgiveness. It's a shame to be mad at people when they don't even know you're mad at them. That's a normal thing in today's church.

Because of it, the spirit of offense is catapulting to new heights like never before. *Scandalon* is the Greek word for "offense." It also means a rat trap—not the whole trap, but the trigger part of the trap that you put the cheese on. The scandalon traps a person because he cannot forgive, thus causing God not to forgive him and ultimately causing great loss. That's why you noticed that God tells us in Luke 17:1 that offenses will come, but if they are handled according to Jesus' teaching, we will not get trapped.

Secondly, Jesus says, "and *if* they repent." I believe this is the most important part of forgiveness. We have already taught on repentance in a earlier chapter. It means to turn toward God in thinking and actions. Then God wants us to forgive them. One thing you have to know about God is that he will never ask you to do something he will not do. God will never forgive a sin that has not been repented of. If he won't do it, he will not ask you to. Now I know this is scary to some, but it is the truth. Remember the story about the bank robber asking for mercy and forgiveness as he kept robbing the bank. If a sin is going to be forgiven, you have to stop or repent. Now I know some scholars will say, "No way. God wants us to love everyone." And that is *absolutely* correct. But love and forgiveness are different. When God doesn't forgive us, it doesn't mean he stops loving us. The reason he seeks repentance from us is because he loves us. He never stops loving us. Remember 2 Peter 3:9: "The Lord is not slack concerning his promise, as some men count slackness; but is longsuffering to usward, not willing that any should perish, but that all should come to repentance." God want us to love sinners and pray that they turn toward God, that they may receive a pardon. They don't understand that they are trapped by a rat trap, and only you can release them from this trap. We should love them in every area, as

God loves them, hoping and praying that they repent. You may go ahead and forgive them, but they will still be trapped. In the holy scriptures, there has never been a sin forgiven by God that wasn't repented of.

Jesus says that if they repent, you have to forgive them or give them their ticket to be sent away. This is what the apostles were laboring with: forgiving people even though they have repented. They couldn't imagine forgiving people who had tried to hurt them or slandered their names and Jesus' name. However, Jesus said that even if they do it time after time after time but repent each time, you have to forgive them if you want the father to forgive you. Why would Jesus say such a thing? Because Jesus knew how many times we sinned against God before salvation, and even after salvation. After we repent, God acts like we've done nothing. After all the transgressions and all the iniquities, after repentance, God forgives us, by bankrupting heaven of his only begotten son.

Now remember, in those days, everyone knew that if you wanted to be forgiven, you had to repent. Remember the example of going to Wal-Mart. Repentance was a given if you wanted forgiveness. In today's society, this seems so hard to accomplish or imagine. We have to remember that if we seek God for help, his grace pulls us out of the trap of the enemy. Peter 5:5 says, "For God resisteth the proud, and giveth grace to the humble." God gives strength to those who submit to the word of God. Jesus again builds on Luke 17:3 as a basis for the teaching forgiveness. Let's look at other scriptures that Jesus taught.

In Matthew 6:14–15, Jesus warns us what happens if we don't forgive: "For if ye forgive men their trespasses, your heavenly Father will also forgive you: But if ye forgive not men their trespasses, neither will your Father forgive your trespasses." Jesus is speaking about forgiving someone who has repented. This verses is built around Luke 17, in which repentance is a given. God will never ask you to do something he would never do. So Jesus is saying, after someone sins or offends you, *if* he repents and you deny him a pardon, God will deny you on that day. Some will say, "That's easy; I can do that to assure faring well on that day." But if some pedophile rapes your daughter and the authorities catch him and he vigorously seeks forgiveness after repenting, could you forgive him? Or what if he killed her? Could you honestly say you could forgive him? This could be a difficult matter, but with the grace or strength of God, which he gives to the humble, it can be done. There was once a man who murdered this Christian woman's daughter, and when the man entered the courtroom, he screamed, in tears, "Please forgive me."

The woman yelled, "I will never forgive you, and I pray you burn in hell." After the trial, the man was found guilty and sentenced to death. The woman was glad he got what he deserved.

The woman's pastor comforted her the best he could, but there was so much hatred in her. Finally, her pastor told her, "You have to forgive him if you want to be forgiven for your sins." She stated she would never forgive him.

Years later, when the man was laid on the gurney for his lethal injection, she asked for a front-row seat. She wanted to see him pay for his deeds. As they pressed the button for injection, the man made eye contact with the woman and asked for the last time, "Please forgive me."

With tears running down her face, the woman said, "I do

forgive you." The man died, and the woman came to find out he had received Christ in prison.

These truths that Christ taught are huge. This task cannot be done unless God gives a person grace or strength. There is a hurt that is so overbearing that only through Jesus can we forgive. We have to remember that God bankrupted heaven that our sins may be forgiven—all of them. God knows that if he can forgive every one of our dirty, filthy, and selfish sins, we should be able to forgive each other.

Luke 7:47 says, "Wherefore I say unto thee, 'Her sins, which are many, are forgiven; for she loved much: but to whom little is forgiven, the same loveth little.'" Mary had probably heard Jesus speaking in the streets, and she followed him to the Pharisee's house. Normally, such a task would be prohibited, but she was on a mission. It's something when you receive a word from Jesus. So, she eased in unnoticed until she stood behind Jesus as he conversed with the men. While Jesus was speaking, she fell at Jesus' feet and started crying, washing his feet with her tears. Then she took her hair, because there was not a towel, and dried his feet with her hair. All of this love was for the forgiveness of so many of her sins. No matter what was done to Mary, she would have forgiven it. Why? Because God forgave her. God did it to a much higher degree, and he expects us to at least forgive at our humanly lower degree. God expects us to have a heart like Mary's. We had many sins forgiven, so we must love. Let's look at Jesus' other teachings on forgiveness.

In Matthew 18:21–22, it says, "Peter came to Jesus, and said, 'Lord, how oft shall my brother sin against me, and I forgive him? Till seven times?' Jesus saith unto him, 'I say not unto thee, Until seven times: but, until seventy times seven.'" This truth is based on the person repenting. Notice in the following parable the servant fell down and worshipped him, saying, "Lord, have patience with me, and I will pay thee all." This was a type of repentance. "Then the lord of that servant was moved with compassion, and loosed him, and forgave him the debt" (Matthew 18:27). After repentance came, then forgiveness had her way. That is the order of God. Notice the rest of this parable. "But the same servant went out, and found one of his fellow servants, which owed him an hundred pence: and he laid hands on him, and took him by the throat, saying, 'Pay me that thou owest.' And his fellow servant fell down at his feet, and besought him, saying, 'Have patience with me, and I will pay thee all.' And he would not: but went and cast him into prison, till he should pay the debt. So when his fellow servants saw what was done, they were very sorry, and came and told unto their lord all that was done. Then his lord, after that he had called him, said unto him, 'O thou wicked servant, I forgave thee all that debt, because thou desiredst me: Shouldest not thou also have had compassion on thy fellowservant, even as I had pity on thee?' And his lord was wroth, and delivered him to the tormentors, till he should pay all that was due unto him" (Matthew 18:28–34). The Lord forgave all the debt of the man who repented, but this same man who had his debt forgiven would not forgive his fellow servant who repented. The Lord delivered him to the tormentors, till all his debt was paid, and that's forever. God loves forgiveness, and so should we. But before we can forgive, our hearts must be filled with the truth of Jesus. We have been reared to forgive people no matter what they do, but that is *a* truth, not *the* truth. We love them in every instance, never turning them away, because Jesus never turned us away. When we repented, God received us wholeheartedly, no matter what we had done or said. When we stay with the order of God, we cannot go wrong.

Forgiveness is an arsenal that can quiet the enemy. His hope is that when people have sinned, we ignore it. When men and women repent, Satan hopes that we deny them pardon or forgiveness.

David Garland states that, throughout the Corinthian correspondence Paul seeks to build up community (see 1 Cor 12:12–26), that requires taking responsibility for one another, disciplining when necessary, forgiving when appropriate, and never doing anything that might lead to another's eternal ruin (1 Cor 8:7–13).[11] This passage and 1 Cor 5:1–5 reveal how important it is for the Christian community to balance the exercise of firm discipline with compassionate charity toward those who repent. Failure to do plays into the hands of Satan.[12]

Paul emphasizes accountability in the letter of Corinthians. As I stated earlier, offenses are running rampant in the church, and the only answer is God's truth: repentance and forgiveness. When we have this truth in our hearts, our works will follow. And guess who gets the praise and glory? The word, Jesus.

Remember, when a man won't repent and we don't forgive him as the scripture stated, we must love him all the more, just as God loved us even though we were not forgiven because we were still in active sin. The reason we hold back forgiveness is that we must pray that God touches the sinner and turns him to repent and come to Jesus. This is important because I don't want anyone taking this teaching to mean they should not love someone. These scriptures are all about love, the love of God.

Chapter 13
Believing the Truth

It's been asked how the patriarchs stayed the course. Their hearts were filled with the truth, from Moses to Jesus. Their hearts were filled with God. Blessed is the man. "But his delight is in the law of the LORD; and in his law doth he meditate day and night. And he shall be like a tree planted by the rivers of water, that bringeth forth his fruit in his season; his leaf also shall not wither; and whatsoever he doeth shall prosper" (Psalm 1). In this passage, David's delight or trust was in the word. He mediated, reviewing the material, speaking the word to himself. Just like in Romans 10:17, "faith cometh by hearing, and hearing by the word of God." When we read or meditate on the word, then we believe, thus causing this truth to settle in our hearts. Faith is now in our hearts. Our hearts are not only strengthened but filled with the precious love of Jesus.

The men and women of God who were persecuted withstood the hand of the enemy through the word. Let's look at the Book of Hebrews. By believing in the truth, the men and women prevailed in numerous ways. By believing in the truth, the elders were able to obtain a good report. By believing in the truth, Abel was able to offer God an excellent sacrifice. By believing in the truth, Enoch did not see death. By believing in the truth, Noah became heir to the righteousness (works produced by a heart that is filled with truth, which equates to faith). By believing in a truth, Abraham obeyed. By believing in the truth, Moses refused to be called the son of pharaoh's daughter, choosing to suffer affliction with the people of God rather than enjoy the pleasures of sin for a season. All these things happened because some decided to believe *the* truth versus *a* truth. Because they did, they fared well with God on that day. They cannot brag, saying it was their doing; they realize it was the word's doing or Jesus' doing that produced good works.

How the Holy Spirit Influences the Heart

The Holy Ghost is *God in action, God in motion.* God's wisdom is given to us in scripture and understood through the Spirit. I spoke earlier about understanding the word. You have to understand it to believe it. Acts 5:32 states that if you obey God, you will receive the Holy Spirit. The Holy Ghost or Spirit gives us grace (strength) to understand the word of God. When we make a conscious decision to obey God, he gives us his precious gift, the Holy Ghost, and he helps us understand the word. Satan deals with darkness or ignorance. He hides the truth with false truths as discussed earlier. But the Holy Ghost gives us discernment in truth. He enlighten us to God's word, thus causing understanding of the word. Surely the devil doesn't want anyone to receive the Holy Ghost. Satan even tries to make the Spirit of God spooky or so mysterious that many would be afraid and not willing to receive him. "For the kingdom of God are not meat and drink; but righteousness, and peace, and joy in the Holy Ghost" (Romans

14:17). The Holy Ghost brings righteousness and convicts sin. He produces peace in the most miserable places and he presses for unspeakable joy in the believer's heart. This is the kingdom of God at its greatest because the Holy Ghost brings the ways of heaven on earth and in men and women.

The Holy Ghost is the key to God's kingdom because he operates in every born-again believer. He is of paramount importance in shaping the hearts of men and women. He comforts us when the enemy comes in like a flood; he strengthens us with his grace.

Every morning when you wake, you should speak first to the Holy Ghost. He is a person, and he is God. For so long, many men and women of God have taken the Spirit of God for granted, but the Holy Ghost is a person, the third part of the trinity. He appreciates the love we show him. The Holy Ghost has feelings just like you. He hurts, he grieves, and he always gives godly direction. He will not force you to do anything. He always leans to humility and humbleness. But of course, the flesh leans to pride and selfishness. Often, the Holy Ghost warns us of trouble and even directs us to righteous; thus, joy prevails.

There was once in a rural town where a lady was working at an office and something just keep tugging at her spirit to get up and go home. She fought it for an hour or so, thinking, "Why do I need to go home?" Finally, she gave in to that tugging and she headed home. When she got there, she walked in the door and the television was on. She noticed that there was a news alert reporting a shooting. She sat down in front of the television and saw the shooting was at the office she had just left. She started weeping and thanking God for intervening for her. The Holy Ghost is surely a comforter. The Holy Ghost is God; it's just that simple. He never tells you what he wants to tell you, but he always speaks what he hear. Oh, how I love the Holy Ghost. He's not mysterious as some will have you believe, but loving, just as Jesus the Christ was and is. Of course, I don't have the time or the space to write everything about the Holy Ghost, and if you don't have him, please stop right now and ask for him. Luke 11:9–13 states, "And I say unto you, 'Ask, and it shall be given you; seek, and ye shall find; knock, and it shall be opened unto you.' For every one that asketh receiveth; and he that seeketh findeth; and to him that knocketh it shall be opened. If a son shall ask bread of any of you that is a father, will he give him a stone? Or if he ask a fish, will he for a fish give him a serpent? Or if he shall ask an egg, will he offer him a scorpion? If ye then, being evil, know how to give good gifts unto your children: how much more shall your heavenly Father give the Holy Spirit to them that ask him?" God wants you to have him not only outside of you, or externally, but God wants to be inside of you. This is where the change of man occurs.

The Spirit of God is sight, while the word, Jesus, is light. "Thy word is a lamp unto my feet, and a light unto my path" (Psalms 119:105). You can have light without sight. A. W. Tozer once stated that a blind man doesn't have sight, even with a lantern. The Holy Ghost gives the power of sight. As stated earlier, you have to understand to believe. When we really understand the scripture, then our hearts are filled with truth. If not, our hearts can be filled with errors. "Let him know, that he which converteth the sinner from the error of his way shall save a soul from death, and shall hide a multitude of sins" (James 5:20).

In the end time church age, truths are protruding out as new revelations all over the world, in every religion and every country.

Men and women's hearts are at stake. Jesus even reminded us in scriptures about lies and worldly truths. Matthew 24:23–24 states, "Then if any man shall say unto you, 'Lo, here is Christ,' or there; believe it not. For there shall arise false Christs, and false prophets, and shall show great signs and wonders; insomuch that, if it were possible, they shall deceive the very elect." Jesus is talking about the ones who will accept him as their savior during the awful tribulation years. The lies and false truths literally cover the earth. The Holy Ghost will be the only one who will discern between good and evil. This is the very reason to survive in the last days. You will have to have the precious Holy Ghost.

Chapter 14
How to Receive the Holy Ghost

Normally, when people see such a topic, they get excited because they think it's like a cook book or a manual for putting a bike together. Do a little of this and a little of that for easy directions to the Holy Ghost. Well, I'm sorry, that is not what this is. It is simply what scripture states about receiving him. I'm going to state some things A. W. Tozer wrote about receiving the Holy Ghost. You probably already know, but just in case, here it is. This is how to receive God's precious Holy Ghost. First, present your body to him (Rom 12:1–2). God can't fill what he can't have. Now I ask you, are you ready to present your body with all of its functions and all that it contains—your mind, your personality, your spirit, your love, your ambitions, your all? That is the first thing. You may say, "That not's difficult at all. That is a simple, easy act—presenting the body." Are you willing to do it?

Now the second thing is to *ask* (Luke 11:9–11), and I set aside all theological objections to this text. They say that is not for today. Well, why did the Lord leave it in the Bible then? Why didn't he put it somewhere else? Why did he put it where I could see it if he didn't want me to believe it? If the Lord wanted to, he could give it without our asking, but he chooses to have us ask.

"Ask of me, and I will give thee" is always God's order, so why not ask?

Acts 5:32 tells us the third thing to do. God gives his Holy Spirit to those who obey him. I covered that already a few chapters back. Are you ready to obey and do what you are asked to do? What would that be? Simply to live by the scriptures as you are taught them. How can we hear unless there is a preacher? Rom 10:14 states, "How can we understand unless we are guided or taught?" Acts 8:31 says, "And he said, 'How can I, except some man should guide me?'"

The next thing is, have faith (Gal 3:2). We receive him through faith as we receive the Lord in salvation through faith. He comes to us as a gift of God in power. First, he comes in some degree and measure when we are converted; otherwise, we couldn't be converted. Without him, we couldn't be born again, because we are born of the Spirit. But I am talking about something different now. I am talking about his coming and possessing the full body and mind and life and heart, taking the whole personality over, gently, but directly and bluntly, and making it his, so that we may become a habitation of God through the Spirit.

Conclusion

I pray that not only has your outlook toward yourself changed, but also your outlook toward Jesus (the word, the truth). If it has, God bless you all the more as you reread this book, until God shows you your purpose and plan for your life. That's right: reread it and get it in your heart and spirit like never before. Each time you read it, God will give you more and more revelation. Now, let's list a few short points to remember.

The spiritual heart is not in your chest but between your ears. The world, Satan, you, and Jesus all strive to win your heart. There is continuous war over your heart, and whoever wins will control you.

There are many truths, but there is just one truth: Jesus.

The heart is a *holder of truths* as you know them to be true. False truths are all through the land, seducing the heart at every opportunity.

True salvation is based on a person's heart. Whatever is in the heart, the body performs or works out. This is why Jesus speaks so often about works in the New Testament.

Forgiveness is an integral part of the kingdom of God and must be strived after continuously.

Repentance is the key to the heart of God, and there has never been a biblically recorded sin that was forgiven that was not was repented of.

Bibliography

Garland, David E. *2 Cor.* Nashville, TN: Broadman & Holman Publishers, 2001. Electronic edition.

Strong, James. *The Exhaustive Concordance of the Bible: Showing Every Word of the Text of the Common English Version of the Canonical Books, and Every Occurrence of Each Word in Regular Order.* Ontario: Woodside Bible Fellowship, 1996. Electronic edition.

The Holy Bible: King James Version. Bellingham, WA: Logos Research Systems, Inc., 1995. Electronic edition.

Walvoord, John F. and Roy B. Zuck. *The Bible Knowledge Commentary: An Exposition of the Scriptures.* Wheaton, IL: Victor Books, 1985.

Zodhiates, Spiros. *The Complete Word Study Dictionary: New Testament.* Chattanooga, TN: AMG Publishers, 2000. Electronic edition.

Endnotes

1. Spiros, *The Complete Word Study Dictionary: New Testament.*
2. Strong, *The Exhaustive Concordance of the Bible.*
3. Walvoord, *The Bible Knowledge Commentary.*
4. *The Holy Bible: King James Version.*
5. Strong, *The Exhaustive Concordance of the Bible.*
6. Strong, *The Exhaustive Concordance of the Bible.*
7. Strong, *The Exhaustive Concordance of the Bible.*
8. Walvoord, *The Bible Knowledge Commentary.*
9. Strong, *The Exhaustive Concordance of the Bible.*
10. Strong, *The Exhaustive Concordance of the Bible.*
11. Garland, *2 Cor.*
12. Garland, *2 Cor.*